Fat
Burning
FOODS

and other weight-loss secrets

Fat
Burning
FOODS
and other weight-loss secrets

By Judy Jameson

Ottenheimer
PUBLISHERS

CONTENTS

INTRODUCTION

CONGRATULATIONS! You've just taken the first step towards easy, permanent weight loss. Being concerned about those extra pounds will be a thing of the past after you discover fat-burning foods and learn other weight-loss secrets. The following new discoveries in weight loss can make you more slender and energetic than ever before!

➤ Foods high in **complex carbohydrates** are not only satisfying, they are an extraordinary fat-burning tool.

➤ The amount of **fat** you eat, not total calories, will determine whether or not you gain weight.

➤ Simple, moderate **exercise** on a regular basis will keep your metabolism high enough to ensure maximum fat-burning.

➤ Slow and steady wins the weight-loss race. When you continue to lose at a rate of two pounds a week, **you'll keep those pounds off.**

➤ Losing weight is **good** for your health! This program will cut your risk of contracting such life-threatening diseases as cancer, heart disease, and high blood pressure.

Best of all, this program is incredibly easy to follow. It involves no calorie-counting, no complicated calculations, and no specialized foods or food combinations. It also promises you no more hunger pangs and no more growly stomach. In fact, **you will not be hungry during this program!**

Your 30 Miracle Foods

This amazing program is based on 30 "miracle" foods high in complex carbohydrates. Foods such as rice, potatoes, and pastas, as well as fruits and vegetables, are not only nutritious, satisfying, and inexpensive. They're also high in fiber and may well reduce your exposure to diseases such as cancer. You'll learn how these foods, when combined with simple exercise, will actually "teach" your body to burn fat and lose weight.

Here's a list of 30 fat-burning foods you can eat until you're fully satisfied.

Apples
Bananas
Beans (all varieties)
Bread (plain)
Broccoflower
Broccoli
Cabbage
Cauliflower
Celery
Citrus fruit
Corn, including air-
   popped popcorn
Cranberries
Frozen low-fat waffles
   and pancakes
Grains and grain products
Grapes

Jam (sugar-free, low-cal
   only)
Leeks
Lettuce
Melon
Mushrooms
Pasta (low-fat, preferably
   whole grain)
Pears
Peas
Peppers
Pineapple
Potatoes
Root vegetables
Spinach
Tomatoes
Zucchini

In the pages ahead, you'll learn about studies that prove your body handles complex carbohydrates differently than it does other types of food. Complex carbohydrates seem to lose many of their calories as they're being digested. That means you can eat until you're completely satisfied—and still lose weight!

But, of course, one cannot live by bread alone. This program also includes moderate amounts of protein (eggs, low-fat cheese, fish, and chicken) and very low amounts of fat, especially saturated fats (the kind found in red meat and butter).

Another key step towards a successful slimdown is cutting down on fats. Scientists have discovered that fat actually hangs on to its calories while moving through your body. Again, you'll learn more details in the pages ahead. For now, just remember that calories from fat in foods are more likely to "stick to your waistline" than calories from carbohydrates and protein.

Finally, you'll learn that food alone won't do the trick. Regular activity brings your metabolism high enough to keep the fat-burning action going. This book will provide you with practical tips on exercise that you can easily incorporate into your life. They're an essential component of this program.

Why Diets Don't Work

Americans are just plain diet crazy. And yet, most diets don't work. Believe it or not, over one-third of American women and a quarter of a million American men are dieting each day. Yet, more than 90 percent of these diets will be unsuccessful.

By now, you've probably tried a grapefruit diet, a food-combining diet, a Scarsdale diet, a liquid diet . . . the list goes on and on. You've weighed every morsel of food that went into your mouth for weeks at a time, or you've counted calories until your calculator went on the fritz. You may have tried "diet pills," which suppressed your appetite and kept you awake all night. Or diuretics, which made you lose water and salt, not fat. Or laxatives, which may have damaged your digestive system and seriously risked your health. Or hormones, which may have created a wide range of physical problems.

What did you achieve? Chances are, you ended up with a thicker waistline and wider hips than you had before!

The fact is, "fad-of-the-month" diets cause you more harm than good, mostly because they suddenly deprive your body of food. When your body thinks it's starving, your survival instinct kicks in and tries to preserve your fat stores to maintain the status quo.

As your hunger continues, your body reacts to "starvation" by decreasing its *basal metabolic rate* (the rate at which your body burns calories) in order to conserve energy. Your body becomes super-efficient at storing whatever calories it doesn't use as body fat. The less you eat, the harder your body tries to retain fat.

Then, when you go off one of the diets—and eventually you'll want to eat "normally" again—not only will you gain all the weight back, but you'll likely end up heavier than before.

It's a vicious cycle—one that puts you back at square one every time. The only permanent loss you might experience is in your bank account. Have you ever noticed that fad diets or pills are not cheap?

The fat-burning foods approach is completely different. One of the most important keys to success in this exciting new program is that you're not going to be hungry. Whenever you feel the urge to munch, you can grab one of the 30 fat-burning foods and eat until you're satisfied. Your body never "starves," so your basal metabolic rate stays high and you keep burning off extra fat slowly and steadily.

Best of all, this simple program will fill you up with satisfying foods and delicious tastes. You'll learn how your body reacts to fat-burning foods and why they are perfect for easy weight loss. You'll also learn about "diet foes"—foods and other factors that make you gain weight. Best of all, you'll find that making a commitment to good health is easy. Read on to discover . . .

The secret of permanent weight loss: The basic ideas behind this amazingly simple weight-loss and weight-maintenance plan.

The step-by-step plan to a slim new you: A detailed plan for getting started, including essential hints for success, shopping tips, food preparation tips, and an easy-to-begin activity program.

Sure-fire ways to keep excess pounds off: Suggestions for fast meals, eating out, and coping with social situations.

Delicious recipes and tantalizing menus: A seven-day menu and easy-to-prepare recipes feature delicious fat-burning foods to help you enjoy taking off those pounds.

A Word of Caution

Following this program will improve your health. But before making changes to your diet or activity level, it's always wise to discuss your decision with your physician. This book is designed to *supplement* your physician's prescribed treatment, not replace it.

CHAPTER 1

THE SECRET OF PERMANENT WEIGHT LOSS

Why You Need to Lose Weight— Starting Right Now!

IF YOU'RE READING THIS BOOK, you're probably tired of carrying extra weight. It's discouraging to find your clothes getting tight, and shunning your image in the mirror.

Carrying extra weight is also a major health risk. If you're overweight, you probably have excess fats in your blood. This builds up in the arteries of your heart, leading to angina and heart attacks. Obesity also strains your heart, which is forced to pump blood through all the extra arteries your body grows to feed your fat deposits.

Furthermore, if you are suffering from diabetes, high triglycerides, or high blood pressure, you can't afford to be even moderately overweight. A portly frame can result in hypertension, cardiovascular disease, gallbladder disease, diabetes, and some types of cancers. **Obesity can kill you. But losing weight can reduce and ultimately eliminate that potential!**

Test your weight-loss savvy

True or false?

1. Foods labeled "cholesterol-free" or "no cholesterol" are better for weight loss than other products.
2. Foods that have one of the new labels stating they're "light" or "lite" are ideal for weight-loss programs.
3. Vegetable oils or margarine are better for weight loss than butter.
4. Lasagna and other pasta products are too fattening for any weight-loss diet.
5. Half a croissant is less fattening than a large plate of rice.
6. Dairy products are always fattening.
7. If you really want to lose weight, eliminate red meat.
8. Chicken is a good source of dietary fiber.
9. A lean cut of beef is always bright red.
10. If you really want to lose weight, eat a lot of cheese.

All false. Here's why:

1. *False.* All vegetable oils, for instance, are "cholesterol-free." They're still all fat, and should be avoided.
2. *False.* "Light" could refer to less sugar or salt, or less of a particular nutrient than that contained in the regular version. The words "lite" or "light" may even describe its color, taste, or texture. Current FDA regulations stipulate, however, that if the label "lite" or "light" describes fat content, the food must have one-third fewer calories, or 50 percent less fat, than the standard version.
3. *False.* Vegetable oils and margarine are equally fattening.

4. *False.* Pasta is an excellent diet food. It's when you load it up with high-fat cheeses and ground beef that you add pounds and inches.

5. *False.* Croissants are approximately 45 percent fat. Rice is more filling and satisfying, and has only trace amounts of fat.

6. *False.* Although you can't eat unlimited amounts of milk and cheese, you can get your calcium and protein from skim milk, low-fat yogurt, and low-fat cheeses. These should be eaten in limited quantities.

7. *False.* Red meat is a good source of protein. You can eat small amounts of beef, pork, and chicken, and still lose weight.

8. *False.* There's no dietary fiber in meat or in dairy products. Dietary fiber derives from plants.

9. *False.* Lean beef has very little marbling and white fatty bits; the color of the beef itself does not indicate leanness.

10. *False.* Most hard cheeses are high in fat.

Risky business

Now that you've evaluated your weight-loss savvy, the next step is to determine whether your excess pounds are putting you at risk for serious health problems. Here's how:

A. Enter your current weight: _____ pounds
B. Find your ideal weight, according to Metropolitan Life Insurance Company's chart on page 11: _____ pounds
C. Subtract your ideal weight (B) from your current weight (A): _____ – _____ = _____
        A   B   C

D. Multiply difference (C) by 100:

_____ x 100 = _____ %
   C   D

If D is greater than 25 to 30 percent, those extra pounds you're carrying may be affecting your health.

Another method to determine whether your excess pounds are putting your health at risk is to calculate your Body Mass Index (BMI) and your Waist-Hip Ratio.

The BMI, the ratio of your weight to your height, is most useful for people ages twenty to sixty-five. It is not appropriate for very muscular people, endurance athletes, or pregnant or nursing women. Here's how to figure your BMI using the chart on page 13.

1. On line A, mark an X at your height.
2. On line B, mark an X at your weight.
3. With a ruler, join the two Xs.
4. Extend the line with the ruler to line C. This is your BMI.

If you have a BMI higher than 27, you are probably overweight. You are more likely to develop problems such as heart disease or high blood pressure than someone whose BMI falls below that range.

A high BMI alone does not necessarily mean you need to lose weight. The amount of fat you have and where it is distributed on your body is the other critical factor. If your body resembles an "apple" rather than a "pear," you may be at increased risk of health problems.

STANDARD METROPOLITAN LIFE INSURANCE HEIGHT/WEIGHT TABLES

Women

Height Feet	Inches	Small Frame*	Medium Frame	Large Frame
4	10	102–111	109–121	118–131
4	11	103–113	111–123	120–134
5	0	104–115	113–126	122–137
5	1	106–118	115–129	125–140
5	2	108–121	118–132	128–143
5	3	111–124	121–135	131–147
5	4	114–127	124–138	134–151
5	5	117–130	127–141	137–155
5	6	120–133	130–144	140–159
5	7	123–136	133–147	143–163
5	8	126–139	136–150	146–167
5	9	129–142	139–153	149–170
5	10	132–145	142–156	152–173
5	11	135–148	145–159	155–176
6	0	138–151	148–162	158–179

Men

Height Feet	Inches	Small Frame	Medium Frame	Large Frame
5	2	128–134	131–141	138–150
5	3	130–136	133–143	140–153
5	4	132–138	135–145	142–156
5	5	134–140	137–148	144–160
5	6	136–142	139–151	146–164
5	7	138–145	142–154	149–168
5	8	140–148	145–157	152–172
5	9	142–151	148–160	155–176
5	10	144–154	151–163	158–180
5	11	146–157	154–166	161–184
6	0	149–160	157–170	164–188
6	1	152–164	160–174	168–192
6	2	155–168	164–178	172–197
6	3	158–172	167–182	176–202
6	4	162–176	171–187	181–207

*See page 12 to determine frame size.

STANDARD METROPOLITAN LIFE INSURANCE ELBOW MEASUREMENTS FOR MEDIUM FRAME

* To determine your frame size, bend your forearm upward at a 90 degree angle. Keep fingers straight and turn the inside of your wrist toward your body. Place thumb and index finger of other hand on the two prominent bones on either side of the elbow. Measure space between your fingers on a ruler. Compare with the tables below listing medium-framed men and women. Measurements lower than those listed indicate small frame. Higher measurements indicate large frame.

Height in 1" Heels	Elbow Breadth
Women	
4'10"–5'3"	2 $1/4$"–2 $1/2$"
5'0"–5'3"	2 $1/4$"–2 $1/2$"
5'4"–5'7"	2 $3/8$"–2 $5/8$"
5'8"–5'11"	2 $3/8$"–2 $5/8$"
6'0"	2 $1/2$"–2 $3/4$"
Men	
5'2"–5'3"	2 $1/2$"–2 $7/8$"
5'4"–5'7"	2 $5/8$"–2 $7/8$"
5'8"–5'11"	2 $3/4$"–3"
6'0"–6'3"	2 $3/4$"–3 $1/8$"
6'4"	2 $7/8$"–3 $1/4$"

Source: 1979 Build Study, Society of Actuaries and Association of Life Insurance Medical Directors of America, 1980. Copyright 1983, 1993 Metropolitan Life Insurance Company.

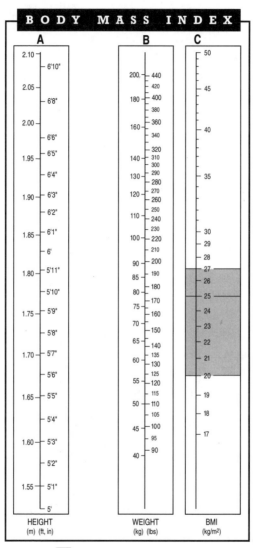

generally acceptable range

Source: Health Canada, 1991. Reproduced with permission of the Minister of Supply and Services Canada 1995.

To determine whether you're an "apple" or a "pear," calculate your Waist-Hip Ratio. Here's how:

A. Measure the circumference of the smallest part of your waist: _____ inches
B. Measure the circumference of the widest part of your hip: _____ inches
C. Divide your waist measurement (A) by your hip measurement (B) to get your Waist-Hip Ratio (C):

$$\underset{A}{\underline{\hspace{2cm}}} \div \underset{B}{\underline{\hspace{2cm}}} = \underset{C}{\underline{\hspace{2cm}}}$$

Your health is at increased risk due to excess weight if C, your Waist-Hip Ratio, is 1.0 or greater (for men), or 0.8 or greater (for women).

The Calorie-Counting Game

Starvation diets don't work because you need nourishment just to stay alive. The energy from food—calories—provides your body with the energy it needs to breathe, to keep your blood pumping, and to carry on other important life functions.

On other diets, you probably spent hours calculating the calories in your food. According to the theory, calories are the basic unit of energy that food can provide. The higher the calories in a particular food, the more energy it contains. This energy can fuel your body's basic functions. But, if calories are not burned off, they can accumulate as unwanted fat.

According to the Food and Nutrition Board, the average American adult male of 154 pounds requires between 1,440 to

1,728 calories a day—just to lie around! The average inactive female of 128 pounds uses up 1,296 to 1,584 calories a day. So most conventional diets tell you to consume fewer calories than you need, and supposedly, you'll lose weight.

Wrong! If calories alone made you overweight, Americans would all be thin. Believe it or not, we actually consume fewer calories now than we did 100 years ago. The difference between then and now, however, is more than just calorie consumption. A century ago, people were far more physically active. They also ate no processed foods, which tend to be high in sugar and fat.

In theory, the fewer calories you eat, the more weight you lose. But that theory won't work if you have a relatively low basal metabolic rate. As you've already learned, when you starve yourself your system copes by dropping your basal metabolic rate. Starvation dieting makes your body hang on to every bit of body fat it can. **That's why starvation diets are the worst possible solution for an overweight person.**

Ideally, your diet should contain at least 10 calories per pound of your ideal body weight. In other words, if you want to weigh 120 pounds, you should be eating at least 1,200 calories every day. But nobody wants to count calories, and that leads us to the beauty of this program.

By eating fat-burning foods and keeping up your physical activity, your body will use up your calories **before** they turn to fat. So put away your calorie counter and read on.

Pyramids and the Power of Three

The U.S. Department of Agriculture's (USDA) new Food Guide Pyramid provides a practical set of eating guidelines for

FOOD GUIDE PYRAMID

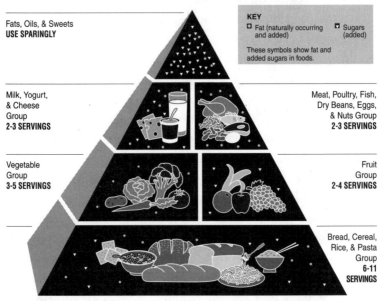

Source: U.S. Department of Agriculture/U.S. Department of Health and Human Services

all Americans. At the base of the pyramid—the foundation of every good diet—the USDA recommends 6 to 11 daily servings of grain-based foods (bread, cereal, rice, and pasta). The second most important food groups, one tier up, are vegetables (3 to 6 servings) and fruit (2 to 4 servings). The next level is shared by milk, yogurt, and cheese (2 to 3 servings) as well as meat, poultry, dry beans, eggs, and nuts (2 to 3 servings). At the top point of the pyramid are fats, oils, and sweets that are to be used sparingly.

The truth is, only three kinds of foods provide your body with the calories it needs to sustain life: carbohydrates, fats, and proteins. We will discuss each of these.

Complex Carbohydrates: Nature's Fat-Burners

Next to water, your body needs more carbohydrates than any other nutrient. Doctors and nutritionists say carbohydrates are invaluable sources of these nutrients:

Iron	Vitamin A	Magnesium
Phosphorous	Vitamin B6	Iodine
Thiamine	Vitamin C	Folacin
Niacin	Copper	Protein

There are two kinds of carbohydrates: *simple* and *complex.* *Simple carbohydrates* include jelly beans and sugary soft drinks. They're generally low in nutritional value. Complex carbohydrates, on the other hand, include pasta, potatoes, broccoli, bran, and rice. These provide more even-burning fuel than simple carbohydrates. They're also packed with more nutrients and fiber. They're key players in a successful fat-burning program.

FAT-BURNING FOOD TIP #1

- -

At least 65 percent of the calories in your diet should come from carbohydrates, preferably complex carbohydrates.

In general, *complex carbohydrates* are a happy union of natural sugars, starches, and fiber. They include:

➤ *Sugars,* primarily sucrose, glucose, and fructose, found in fruits, sugar, honey, most syrups, and molasses.

➤ *Starches,* found in bread, pasta, rice, potatoes, and cereals.

➤ *Dietary fiber,* found in whole grains, whole grain products, fruits, vegetables, nuts, seeds, and legumes (seeds of plants such as lentil, pea, and bean).

Ounce for ounce, these foods provide the same amount of energy as protein, yet have fewer than **half** the calories of fat. For every gram of carbohydrate or protein you eat, you get about 4 calories of energy, a considerable savings over the 9 calories you get from fats.

ENERGY FROM FOOD

1 gram of carbohydrate = approximately 4.5 calories of energy
1 gram of protein = approximately 4 calories of energy
1 gram of fat = approximately 9 calories of energy

The bulk of your diet should come from complex carbo-hydrates. These are the ideal fat-burning foods. Because complex carbohydrates break down easily into glucose (blood sugar)—a main source of energy—they are like high-octane, clean-burning fuel for your body.

In addition, although you don't need to count calories on this program, fruits, vegetables, grains, breads, and cereals don't have a lot of calories. You can eat as much as you want of these foods to satisfy your appetite. In fact, your appetite is "cued" to

Carol Kaufman: Crazy for Protein

AT FORTY-THREE, Carol had been on every diet that came along, and she was *still* 30 pounds overweight. Although she loved bread, rice, and potatoes, she was afraid to eat them because she thought these foods were fattening.

Of course, she paid no attention to the fact that she enjoyed her favorite foods with a generous dollop of fat. She always applied a thick layer of butter or mayonnaise to sandwiches. Likewise, she buried baked potatoes under a mound of sour cream.

In fact, she enjoyed rich foods so much that she decided a high-protein approach was the way to lose weight. So her breakfast consisted of eggs and bacon. Lunch was cold cuts, more eggs, and cheese slices. Dinner was meat, meat, and more meat, accompanied by a salad topped with dressing.

She did lose weight at first. But her doctor was not happy when Carol's cholesterol level shot through the roof. Eventually, Carol wasn't happy, either. A month into her high-protein regimen, Carol was constantly fatigued and frequently constipated.

Fortunately, Carol decided to give carbohydrates another chance. But this time, she decided to use good old common sense. For breakfast, she ate bread, jam, fruit, and cereal. For lunch, she filled up with a huge bowl of noodle soup. At dinner, she splurged on two baked potatoes (topped with low-fat sour cream), a small portion of broiled chicken, microwaved vegetables, and a salad splashed with low-fat dressing. Fruit and air-popped popcorn saw her through snack times.

Much to her amazement, Carol lost three pounds the first week. She felt so good that she started looking forward to a half-hour morning walk. The second week, another two pounds disappeared, and she maintained a steady loss of one to two pounds a week for the next few months.

Today Carol is slim, active, and very proud of herself. She hasn't lost her craving for bread, rice, and potatoes; now, she knows they're good for her!

tell your body to stop eating while your body converts energy from carbohydrates into glucose for energy.

A menu loaded with carbohydrates is chock-full of wonderful fat-burning foods. As far back as 1975, Dr. Olaf Michelsen, professor of nutrition at Michigan State University, made a surprising discovery. He found that bread—and lots of it—can be the ideal diet food. A published study demonstrated that overweight young men lost weight easily on a menu that included 12 slices of bread a day! Within eight weeks, the eight men who were given high-fiber bread lost almost 20 pounds, on average. The eight who ate low-fiber bread lost less—13.7 pounds. But they all lost weight, even though they were filling up on bread.

More recently, in 1981, University of Virginia scientists fed adult laboratory rats food identical in calorie and fat content. Some, however, had diets rich in carbohydrates, while others had diets rich in protein. The animals on the carbohydrate-rich diets gained much less weight and put on considerably less body fat than those on diets rich in protein. One of the researchers' explanations was that on a high-carbohydrate, low-protein diet, more calories may be "burned up" as body heat while fewer are stored as energy reserves, or fat.

How can this be? The most likely explanation is that **meals high in complex carbohydrates raise the metabolic rate of overweight people more than meals containing the same number of calories, but composed mostly of fats or proteins.**

Scientists have many theories about why complex carbohydrates have such a magical effect on our weight. One theory is that fat consumption changes your body chemistry to slow down your metabolism. Another theory is that fatty foods somehow interfere with your body's ability to use its fat stores for energy.

Still another theory is that when you eat foods high in complex carbohydrates, you tend to eat enough calories to provide the energy you need. When you eat fatty foods, on the other hand, you are eating for pleasure, rather than for energy. Eating chocolate cake for no other reason than because it tastes good has nothing to do with hunger or your energy requirements.

Other research by Dr. Michael Levitt at Minneapolis Veterans Administration Hospital has shown that up to one-third of the calories in starchy foods are not absorbed by the human body. He suggests that bacteria in the gut "digest" them and eliminate them as gas.

The most compelling theory is that your body seems to "prefer" complex carbohydrates to fats, for energy. One research team, for instance, learned that the body had to use 28 percent of its high-carbohydrate calories to convert them into fat. But the body only had to use 7 percent of its dietary fat calories to convert *them* into fat. Doctors from Stanford University School of Medicine found that complex carbohydrates appear to lose up to one quarter of their calories while being digested. Fat, on the other hand, loses only 3 percent of its calories as it moves through your body (and settles on your waist).

Obviously, it's "easier" for the body to convert carbohydrates into energy and dietary fat into body fat for future use. Perhaps dietary fat is so similar in chemical composition to our body fat that it just takes less energy to convert it into flab.

Whatever theory you choose, two important facts are clear:

➤ **Calories from starch, sugar, and other carbohydrates are not stored in your body as easily as calories from fat.**

➤ **Your body prefers to fuel itself with carbohydrate calories.**

Fill up on fiber!

Complex carbohydrates are essential for another very important reason. These foods are a good source of dietary fiber—the part of the plant which is not digested or is only partially digested by our enzymes.

There are two main types of dietary fiber: *water-soluble* and *insoluble*. Both are excellent for weight control and are superb for your health.

Water-soluble fiber can dissolve in water. It's found in foods such as oat bran, white beans, and many legumes, fruits, and vegetables. In general, these foods help regulate blood sugar levels and may also lower cholesterol in your blood. The soluble fiber in apples and oats has also been linked to reduced risk of heart disease.

How do water-soluble fibers do this? Oat bran appears to form a gel-like substance in the intestines that binds with bile acids. These acids are manufactured by your body's cholesterol stores for use in digesting cholesterol. When you eat a food like oat bran that contains water-soluble fibers, the indigestible fiber attaches itself to the bile acids that carry cholesterol. The whole mass then passes right through your body.

Insoluble fiber is found in foods like wheat bran, lima beans, peanuts, and many legumes, fruits, and vegetables. It provides the roughage your digestive system needs to stay healthy, acting like a toothbrush on the interior of your digestive tract. This action reduces your risk of developing constipation, hemorrhoids, diverticular disease, and possibly some cancers. Eating insoluble fiber in wheat bran has been linked to reduced risk of colon cancer and possibly breast cancer.

Like other complex carbohydrate foods, fiber helps satisfy

SOLUBLE FIBER CONTENT OF COMMON FOODS

Food	Grams of soluble fiber
Oat bran, $1/3$ cup	2.01
Whole-wheat bread, 1 slice	0.34
White rice, raw, $1/6$ cup	0.25
Garbanzo beans, canned, $1/7$ cup	0.16
Kidney beans, canned, $1/2$ cup	1.45
Lentils, dried, cooked, $1/2$ cup	0.56
Navy beans, dried, cooked, $1/2$ cup	2.29
Pinto beans, canned, $1/2$ cup	1.10
Broccoli, frozen, $1/2$ cup	0.98
Potato, white, raw, $1/2$ cup	0.77
Apple, raw, 1 small	0.97
Orange, California seedless navel, 1 small	1.13

hunger, and thus helps you resist the temptation to overload on fat. Fiber in your diet adds necessary bulk and is satisfying. It also takes a long time to chew most fibrous foods, which allows time for the "I'm full" signal to reach your brain.

Furthermore, the fiber in complex carbohydrates absorbs water and slows down the speed at which your stomach can empty itself of food, staving off hunger pangs. The longer the food stays in your stomach, the longer you will feel full.

High-fiber foods also help keep your blood sugar level stable, which makes you feel full and less inclined to keep on eating. The American Physicians' Association has found that fibers in whole grains, some fruits, and vegetables keep sugars in the intestinal tract for longer periods. This makes your blood glucose level go up much slower than if you ate a simple sugar. Your blood glucose level also takes longer to drop down to the lower level again.

As well, high-fiber foods keep your insulin levels stable. Your body releases insulin after you eat. The more food you consume at one sitting, the more insulin your body releases. Insulin is a hormone that encourages your body to burn carbohydrates for energy. It also prevents your body's fat cells from breaking down their fat; indeed, it encourages these cells to "plump up" with the fat you've eaten. So it's a good idea to eat small, high-fiber meals during the day to keep insulin levels low and stable. By doing this, you will burn more carbohydrates and store less fat.

BEST SOURCES OF FIBER

Fruits (fresh, not canned)
Vegetables (fresh, not canned)
Legumes (lentils, beans, and peas)
Nuts or seeds
Whole grains
Whole-grain products

Meet your new best friend—fiber!

What this means, in short, is that you should plan to eat considerably more fiber than you consume now. Thirty to forty grams of fiber is more than double the amount most Americans eat at present.

It's easy to accomplish this if you eat the recommended fat-burning foods. Former diet no-nos like bread, pasta, and cereal will become your new friends. As long as you don't load them up with fat-ridden sauces, fillings, and spreads, or purchase brands that are high in fat, you may fill up on them and still lose weight.

FAT-BURNING FOOD TIP #2

Plan to eat 30 to 40 grams of fiber every day.

To make sure that the breads and cereals you choose are a good source of fiber, read the label and choose those with at least 2, but preferably 4, grams of fiber per serving. Always choose bread made from whole-wheat flour, which has three times as much fiber (1.4 grams per slice) as plain white bread. There's actually very little fiber in white flour or baked goods made with white flour.

You should also start switching your priorities at mealtimes. Instead of protein as dinner's central focus, put the spotlight on carbohydrates, such as pasta or rice dishes. Add at least two vegetables, and enjoy fruit for dessert. You can still eat protein, but consider it an accent, rather than the centerpiece.

If you're adding high-fiber foods to your diet for the first time, it's important to use a variety of sources, and go slow until your system adjusts. Try adding one new high-fiber food per meal for a few days, and then build up your fiber intake from there. Some of these foods can stimulate the formation of intestinal gases, which can make you feel bloated and flatulent until your system adjusts.

It's also essential to drink plenty of fluids. If you consume too much insoluble fiber without drinking enough water to carry it along, the fiber will become dry and constipating.

Satisfying Your Sugar Tooth

SUGAR, BELIEVE IT OR NOT, will not make you gain weight. As a matter of fact, studies indicate that overweight people eat less sugar than lean people do. Although obesity has increased some five-fold in the past forty years, sugar consumption has remained constant.

This doesn't mean you should stuff yourself with jujubes or sugary candies, which are made of refined and/or processed sugars and have no nutritional value (they're also terrible for your teeth). Sugar alone makes your blood glucose level go up very fast and drop just as fast, leaving you as hungry as you were before.

Instead, enjoy the natural simple sugars in apples, grapes, pineapple, and other fruit, which provide vitamins and minerals along with fiber, to satisfy your hunger. Eat as much of them as you like. But the odd sugary treat won't hurt your weight loss, as long as the sugars are not accompanied by fat. Cake, cookies, brownies, and chocolate bars, all of which are high in fat, will make you gain weight. The occasional vanilla wafer or sugar in your tea will not slow down your weight loss on this program.

Your 30 Fat-Burning Foods

Now that you understand why fat-burning foods are key to losing weight, look over this expanded list of your 30 miracle foods. These fat-burning foods are all high in complex carbohydrates and low in fat, and they keep stomachs full.

Apples
Bananas
Beans (all varieties, fresh, sprouted, and dried)
Bread (plain, preferably whole grain)
Broccoflower
Broccoli
Cabbage
Cauliflower
Celery
Citrus fruit (includes lemons, oranges, grapefruit)
Corn, including air-popped popcorn
Cranberries
Grains and grain products (barley, bran, bulgur, couscous, quinoa, rice, rolled oats, corn tortillas, wheat, high-fiber, low-fat cereals)
Grapes

Jam (sugar-free, low-cal only)
Leeks
Lettuce
Melons
Mushrooms
Pasta (low-fat, preferably whole grain)
Pears
Peas (all types)
Peppers
Pineapple
Potatoes
Root vegetables (beets, carrots, onions, parsley, pumpkins, squash, turnips)
Spinach
Tomatoes (includes salt-free, sugar-free tomato sauce and salsa)
Waffles and pancakes (frozen, low-fat)
Zucchini

Fats: First in Your Mouth, Then on Your Hips

Fats, found in most meats, dairy products, nuts, and grain products, are necessary for your health. They help transport some of the vitamins you need, and are an essential part of your cell membranes, some hormones, and digestive acids. They insulate and cushion your major organs, and regulate your temperature. Fat also makes food taste better and keeps you from getting hungry between meals.

FAT-BURNING FOOD TIP #3

- -

Remember that the more fat you eat, the more likely you are to be overweight—and stay overweight.

Many foods that contain fat also contain other valuable nutrients. Red meat is rich in iron and zinc, for example. Dairy products are your most concentrated source of calcium, necessary for strong bones and teeth as well as nerve and muscle health. So it's foolish to cut fat out of your diet altogether.

Trim your fat intake

The trouble is, you don't need nearly as much fat as you're eating. All you really need to satisfy your body's minimum requirements for fat is the equivalent of a daily teaspoon of canola oil, which is pure, unadulterated polyunsaturated fat. You'll get at least that if you eat the minimum protein recommendations of this program.

Researchers have found that the main difference between overweight and slender people is the amount of fat they eat. The average North American diet is about 35 to 40 percent fat, thanks to our fondness for red meat, fried foods, dairy products, and desserts. Overweight people tend to get 40 percent or more of their calories from such fatty foods. Slim people tend to eat more vegetables, fruits, and grains, which are all low-fat foods.

One recent major study has found that there is no relationship between how many calories people eat (relative to body size) and how likely they are to be fat. Another study, from Stanford University School of Medicine, even found that the fewer calories people eat per pound of body weight, the more likely they are to be fat. But both studies came to a common conclusion: **the more fat that people ate, the more likely they were to be overweight.**

FAT-BURNING FOOD TIP #4

Consume no more than
20 to 30 percent of calories
from fat per day.

FAT CONSUMPTION IS THE CRITICAL FACTOR IN OBESITY. You must reduce your fat intake to 20 to 30 percent of your daily calories, preferably less.

One important reason why fats make you fat is that they are a very "expensive" form of energy for your body: they provide 9 calories per gram, as opposed to the 4 calories per gram you get from proteins and carbohydrates. Ounce for ounce, you take in more than twice as many calories when you eat fats as when you eat carbohydrates.

Furthermore, as you have already learned, your body tends to use up the calories from carbohydrates, and store the fats. Fat calories are harder to burn off than carbohydrates and protein. They're also more readily converted to body fat, since your body prefers to use carbohydrate calories for fuel.

To calculate how much fat you're allowed, remember that each gram of fat contains 9 calories. Now perform the following calculation:

A. Number of calories you usually consume daily: _____
B. To determine the allowable daily amount of calories as fat, multiply the number of daily calories (A) by 30 percent: _____ x 0.3 = _____
   A   B
C. To find out how many grams of fat you're allowed daily, divide the total allowable daily calories from fat (B) by 9 calories: _____ ÷ 9 = _____
   B   C

What this means is that a woman consuming 1,200 calories a day should aim to eat no more than 40 grams of fat daily (preferably less), while a man consuming 1,800 calories may eat 60 grams (preferably less).

Antonia Barnes:
After-the-Baby Fat

ANTONIA NEVER had a weight problem until her son, Ryan, was born. She and her husband, Bill, nicknamed him "the boy who doesn't sleep." Antonia's days and nights were a whirl of feeding and changing.

Leisurely mealtimes with Bill became a thing of the past. At dinnertime, they relied on take-out meals of fried chicken, hamburgers, hot dogs, and burritos. When Bill was at work, breakfast and lunch consisted of whatever Antonia could grab on the fly from the fridge, which was usually leftovers from the previous night's dinner.

By Ryan's first birthday, Antonia was finally starting to get a little rest. Then, she got pregnant with Laurie. Little Laurie was born prematurely. Antonia spent two months after her daughter's birth at the hospital, waiting for opportunities to hold the child. Whenever her baby fell asleep, she'd nip down to the hospital cafeteria and load up on lasagna, noodles Alfredo, and meat loaf soaked in gravy. Between meals, vending machines were a rich source of nuts, chocolate bars, and chips.

By the time Laurie left the hospital, Antonia was 50 pounds heavier than she'd ever been. Discouraged by her weight gain, Antonia decided that she had to make time for herself. Bill agreed to watch the children on Saturday afternoons while Antonia visited friends and gossiped over a huge salad. For quick fixes, Antonia had a bowl of whole-grain cereal topped with fruit. She discovered low-fat lasagna and took up stir-frying with a vengeance.

It took a year, but soon she was back to her original (pre-baby) weight. Best of all, the program was terrific for her marriage. She rejoined Bill and their volleyball cronies on Wednesday nights. Last time we checked in, Bill and Antonia were just about to enjoy a regular evening's half-hour bicycle ride together.

Where fat lurks

Animal fat is the most obvious source of fat in your diet. You must cut down your intake of red meat to a maximum of 5 ounces per serving, no more than twice a week. In fact, the upper limit of your red meat consumption should be one or two dinners of red meat per week. The rest of your meat intake should consist of chicken and fish.

The fat in dairy products is another enemy. You must switch to skim milk and low-fat cheese products, and limit your consumption of them to a maximum of 2 cups of milk, or the equivalent, daily.

Oils, margarine, butter, and other "pure" fats, such as those found in most commercial salad dressings, have no place in this program, either. You'll learn so many healthy alternatives that you'll lose your taste for them in no time.

Although vegetables are one of the mainstays of this program, some vegetables, such as avocados and olives, are loaded with fat and should also be avoided.

For the purposes of this program, you should eat as little fat as possible, from all sources. All fats are bad for your waistline.

"Good" fats versus "bad" fats

First, a quick biology lesson. When you eat foods that contain any kind of fat, that fat is digested and transported through your blood to every cell in your body. Unfortunately, fat doesn't dissolve in blood. Some fat is transported in your blood in the form called "triglycerides." The rest is conveyed via one of three different types of fat-carrying molecules called "lipoproteins"— fats in the form of blood cholesterol. Lipoproteins are

FAT CONTENT OF COMMON FOODS

Food	Grams of fat	Percentage of calories from fat
Apple	—	—
Banana	less than 1	5%
Navy beans, 1/2 cup, boiled	less than 1	4%
Red beans, 1/2 cup, canned	—	—
Light bran bread, 1 slice	less than 1	11%
Pumpernickel bagel, 3" diameter	0.5	3%
Broccoli	—	—
Cabbage	—	—
Cauliflower	—	—
Celery	—	—
Orange	—	—
Grapefruit	—	—
Corn, 1 ear, cooked	1.0	10%
Frozen low-fat waffle	1.0	13%
Rice, brown, long-grain, 1 cup cooked	0.9	5%
Spaghetti, 2 oz.	1.0	4%
Lasagna noodles, 2 oz.	1.0	4%
Couscous, 1/2 cup	—	—
Tortilla, 1 small corn	—	—
1 small wheat	2.0	21%
Seedless Thompson grapes, 1/2 cup	—	—
Jam (sugar-free, low-cal)	—	—
Romaine lettuce, 1/2 cup	—	—
Leeks, 1/2 cup	—	—
Cantaloupe, 1 cup	less than 1	8%
Mushrooms, fresh	—	—
Bartlett pear	1.0	9%

Food	Grams of fat	Percentage of calories from fat
Green peas, $^1/_2$ cup	—	—
Pepper, raw	—	—
Pineapple, fresh, 1 cup	0.66	8%
Baked potato, 1 medium	—	—
Beets, fresh	—	—
Pumpkin, fresh, 1 cup	—	—
Spinach, fresh, 1 cup	—	—
Tomatoes	—	—
Squash, summer or winter	—	—

Approach With Caution!

Food	Grams of fat	Percentage of calories from fat
Top round beef, 3 oz., broiled, lean only	5.0	29%
Eye of round steak, 3 oz., lean only, roasted	5.0	30%
Round tip of beef, 3 oz., lean only, roasted	6.0	35%
Sirloin steak, 3 oz., lean only, broiled	7.0	36%
Tenderloin, 3 oz., broiled, lean only	7.0	38%
Parmesan cheese, 1 tbsp., grated	1.5	59%
Mozzarella cheese, 1 oz.	5.0	64%
Chicken breast, 3 oz. no skin, roasted	3.0	19%
skin on, roasted	7.6	35%
Sole, 3 oz. cooked	1.0	11%
baked with butter	0.6	45%

composed of fat (lipid) encased in protein and other fats.

Three main types of lipoproteins are found in your blood:

➤ *High-density lipoproteins (HDLs):* HDLs are the so-called "good" cholesterol. They benefit your heart because they clean up excess cholesterol from body tissues and take it to the liver for processing and elimination.

➤ *Low-density lipoproteins (LDLs):* LDLs are the so-called "bad" cholesterol. If you have too many of them in your blood, they start depositing cholesterol on the walls of your coronary arteries, which enlarges fatty deposits that are already there.

➤ *Very-low-density lipoproteins (VLDLs):* VLDLs are also not good for you, because they are lipoproteins that eventually turn into "bad" LDLs. When you consume more carbohydrates, alcohol, or protein than you need for energy, your body stores the excess calories as fat, or adipose tissue. VLDL molecules carry excess calories from the liver to the fatty tissue, in the form of fats called triglycerides. Once triglycerides are delivered, what remains of the VLDL molecule is an LDL molecule—the "bad" cholesterol.

Dietary Fats in Food

There's a difference between the types of fat in your food and the lipoprotein molecules that ultimately carry fat through your blood. What's important to understand is that the type of fat in your food has an effect on which type of lipoprotein your blood carries. Which types of fat are less harmful to eat than others? Read on to find out.

FAT-BURNING FOOD TIP #5

Avoid fat in your diet whenever possible.

Saturated fats, also known as hydrogenated fats, raise your "bad" cholesterol level in your blood more than unsaturated fats.

Saturated fats are the solid kind found in meats and dairy products such as butter and cheese. They're also found in hydrogenated or partially hydrogenated margarines, shortenings, peanut butter, and certain tropical vegetable oils, including palm, palm kernel, coconut oil, and coconut butter. The process of hydrogenation is used to turn liquid oils into solid margarine. Margarine, shortening, and many cookies, crackers, chips, and other processed foods are made with hydrogenated or partially hydrogenated vegetable oil.

Furthermore, a report out of Harvard University shows that another fat lurking in margarine and other processed foods could be responsible for 30,000 heart disease deaths annually in the United States. The hydrogenation process apparently creates a new type of fat not found in nature: "trans fat." In the American Journal of Public Health, researchers pointed out that trans fatty acids not only raised the "bad" LDL cholesterol level just like saturated fat, but also lowered the "good" HDL cholesterol.

Dorothy Sobel:
Night Time Pastry Fiend

DOROTHY HAD A TROUBLED ADOLESCENCE. Her family moved frequently, so she had to develop new friendships, from scratch, at a dozen different schools. Her mother didn't enjoy the frequent moves any more than she did. There were frequent fights, and her dad moved out a few times.

Dorothy spent many a sad evening in her bedroom, listening to her parents quarrel and feeling sorry for herself. During those lonely nights, her favorite companions were cookies, cakes, and doughnuts. She would lie in bed, sadly contemplating her solitude, while she stuffed her face.

By the time she hit her twenties, Dorothy was 20 pounds overweight—a huge amount for her petite frame—and lonelier than ever. One New Year's, alone as usual, she made her usual New Year's resolution—to lose weight. This time, however, she read up on fat-burning foods.

Fortunately, Dorothy's daytime eating habits were already healthy. She loved salads, pasta, vegetables, grilled fish, and chicken. The problem was that late-night lonely hour. There was no way she could make it to morning without a few munchies between dinnertime and bedtime.

Her main solution was to eat plenty of air-popped popcorn, sprinkled with a butter substitute. She satisfied her hunger for sweets with fruit and the occasional sugar-free jam sandwich on whole-wheat bread. She also joined a bowling club, getting her out of the house at least once a week. And she made it a priority to take a long walk after dinner.

Within a few months, Dorothy's nights were no longer lonely! She had made a few friends at the bowling club, and some of them were available to keep her company on other evenings, too.

The excess weight slid off in plenty of time for summer swimming. By July, Dorothy was in the water, in a bikini!

FAT-BURNING FOOD TIP #6

**Keep your intake of saturated fats
at or below 10 percent of your daily
calorie intake, and your total
fat consumption at or below
20 to 30 percent of your daily
calorie intake.**

You don't need a drop of saturated fat in your diet for good health, so try to keep these types of fat to an absolute minimum.

Foods High in Saturated Fats

Beef (fattier cuts)
Bologna
Butter
Cakes (most)
Cheese
Chicken (dark meat, skin)
Chips (most)
Chocolate
Coconut butter
Coconut oil
Cookies (most)
Corned beef
Crackers (most)
Cream
Fried foods
Granola
Gravy
Hot dogs
Ice cream
Lamb
Lard
Margarine (hydrogenated)
Milk (whole, 2%, 1%)
Non-dairy creamers
Non-dairy whipped cream
Palm kernel oil
Palm oil
Peanut butter (hydro-
    genated)
Pizza
Popcorn (microwave type,
    buttered)

Pork
Processed meats
Pudding
Quiche
Shortening (hydro-
   genated)

Soybean oil
Turkey (dark meat)
Veal (fattier cuts)
Vegetable oils (hydro-
   genated)
Whipped cream

Unsaturated fats are the liquid type of fat. In general, they're not as harmful to your health as saturated fats. There are four types, mostly found in vegetable products.

1. *Monounsaturated fats,* found in certain vegetable oils such as olive oil and canola oils, not only don't raise blood cholesterol levels, but lower them when they replace saturated fats in your diet. They don't lower the "good" cholesterol, HDL, and therefore are not as bad for your health. But you won't lose weight unless you cut them way back in your diet.

Foods High in Monounsaturated Fats

Beef (leaner cuts)
Canola oil
Chicken
Croissants
Eggs
Nuts (almonds, cashews,
   chestnuts, hazelnuts,
   macadamia, peanuts,
   pecans, pistachio)
Olive oil
Olives

Peanut butter (non-
   hydrogenated)
Peanut oil
Pies (most)
Popcorn (popped in
   vegetable oil)
Pork
Rapeseed oil
Shortening (vegetable)
Veal (leaner cuts)

2. *Polyunsaturated fats,* found in other liquid vegetable oils, such as liquid safflower, canola, corn, soybean, nut, or cottonseed oil, have the same good effect on overall blood cholesterol levels as monounsaturated oils. Again, too much of them is not good for your health. In fact, some studies have shown a link between polyunsaturates and breast cancer.

Foods High in Polyunsaturated Fats

Canola oil	Safflower oil
Corn chips	Salad dressings (most types)
Corn oil	Seeds (pumpkin, sesame,
Cottonseed oil	squash, sunflower)
Mayonnaise	Soybean oil
Nut oil	Soybeans
Potato chips	Tofu

3. *Omega-3 fatty acid,* which is another type of polyunsaturated fat, is the type found in fish oil. It received a lot of attention a few years ago as a cure-all for heart disease. Fish oil may reduce your triglyceride levels, but there's no convincing evidence that it reduces cholesterol levels in your blood. Large doses of fish oil supplements may even increase "bad" cholesterol in people who have high triglyceride levels. Fish, however, contains less fat than many other forms of protein, and it may even help prevent blood clots from forming.

Foods High in Omega-3 Fatty Acid

Bluefish	Haddock
Cod	Herring

Mackerel	Sardines
Mussels	Scallops
Oysters	Trout
Salmon	Whitefish

4. *Dietary cholesterol* in food (which is not the same as the lipoproteins in your blood) is a source of fat that actually has no calories, so it doesn't make you gain weight. Dietary cholesterol, however, still isn't good for you in excess quantities. It is absorbed, circulates in your body, and is then deposited in your blood vessels. Dietary cholesterol is found in foods of animal origin. Egg yolks, butter, lard, whole milk, meat, shellfish, and poultry are particularly high in it. Dietary cholesterol is also found in pastries and cakes made with butter or lard and milk products made with whole milk.

Foods High in Dietary Cholesterol

Butter	Milk (whole)
Chicken	Scallops
Eggs	Shrimp
Lard	Turkey
Lobster	

Protein—Too Much, Too Often

You need some protein in your daily diet. This important nutrient is a major component of muscles, bone, cartilage, skin, brain tissue, blood, lymph, enzymes, and many hormones. In fact, the only body substances that normally lack protein are bile and urine.

Proteins are composed of building blocks called "amino acids." There are twenty amino acids, some of which the body cannot make by itself. You need a new supply of protein every day to repair and build almost all body tissues, and to produce virtually every chemical in your body.

Animal products contain all the essential amino acids, so sources such as meats, poultry, cheese, and eggs provide your body with what is called "complete protein." A complete protein can supply all twenty amino acids in a single serving.

Other sources of protein, including legumes (beans, lentils, and peas), whole grains, and milk and milk products, can be an incomplete source. That doesn't mean animal products are your best source of protein. It does mean, however, that if you cut back on animal sources of protein, you must eat a variety of other proteins every day to ensure you're getting your quota. This is especially important for vegetarians, who do not use meat sources for protein.

FAT-BURNING FOOD TIP #7

- -

A maximum of 10 to 15 percent of your daily calories should come from animal sources of protein.

If your daily intake is 2,000 calories, you need only 200 to 400 calories of protein from animals a day, which you can get from 6 ounces of broiled fish and an ounce or two of cottage cheese. Alternatively, you only need about 1 ounce of protein

Johnny Burston:
Greasy Kid Stuff

JOHNNY ACQUIRED HIS TASTE for fatty foods in college. Before he had graduated, he had a Ph.D. in grease! That included expertise in the merits of many a double-cheese-with-everything-on-it pizza, as well as a diet of french fries, hamburgers, fried chicken, chicken-fried steak, potato chips, and, for roughage, cole slaw drowning in mayonnaise or salads drenched in oil and vinegar.

Fortunately for Johnny's waistline (not to mention his long-term health), he married Jocelyn, a woman who had discovered a few fat-burning secrets on her own.

On their wedding day, Johnny was 40 pounds overweight. Although she loved him as he was, Jocelyn was concerned about the long-term health risks of his excess weight. She was especially concerned once she learned that heart disease ran in Johnny's family. But she realized that Johnny was never going to give up all his old habits completely. She decided that she would come up with fat-burning versions of his usual diet.

To begin with, she began turning out "no-cheese" pizzas, topped with tomato sauce and a wide selection of interesting vegetables. French fries were an interesting challenge: she prepared the potatoes, lightly sprayed them with a small amount of vegetable oil, and broiled them in the oven. Johnny never realized that the "hamburgers" she prepared so lovingly were in fact chicken burgers, broiled in the oven. Fried chicken was easily replaced with spicy grilled chicken. Jocelyn made sure that plenty of celery and carrots were always around to replace the potato chips, and she stocked up on fat-free salad dressing to top Johnny's greens.

Her ingenuity became a standing joke between them. And it still gets plenty of laughs among their friends, now that Johnny can boast about his successful weight loss.

for every 18 pounds of ideal body weight. In other words, a 126-pound woman only needs about 7 ounces of protein a day, while a 162-pound man needs about 9 ounces of protein.

Your diet is unlikely to be deficient in proteins. Most Americans eat a diet that contains too much protein, and certainly too much animal protein. In fact, in America, most of us eat at least twice as much animal protein as we need. And too much protein is almost as hazardous as not enough. Your body cannot store protein, so excess quantities put a strain on your liver and kidneys, the organs that process and eliminate what your body doesn't need. Excess protein also promotes the loss of calcium from bones (which can eventually lead to bone loss, fractures, and osteoporosis).

FAT CONTENT IN COMMON SOURCES OF PROTEIN

Food	Percentage of calories from fat
T-bone steak	80%
Hard cheese	75%
Whole milk	48%
Tuna packed in oil	64%
Filet of sole	10%
Chicken (white and dark), skinless	31%
Peanut butter	66%
Bacon	75% or more
Cream cheese	75% or more
"Extra lean" ground beef	54%

FAT CONTENT IN COMMON SOURCES
OF VEGETABLE PROTEIN

Food	Percentage of calories from fat
Rice	1%
Dried beans	3 to 4%
Rice, brown, long-grain, cooked, 1 cup	5%
Italian pasta salad	7%
Whole-wheat spaghetti with tomato sauce	5%

Too much protein from animal sources will make you gain weight because meats and cheeses—the most common sources—are also high in fat and calories. Remember, animal protein seldom travels "solo." Usually, it takes plenty of fat along for the ride.

You don't have to eliminate steak and roast chicken from your menu. But you can reduce your protein intake relatively painlessly by filling up instead on those healthy, fat-burning complex carbohydrates. Consider replacing high-fat protein with low-fat sources. Dried peas, beans, and many whole grains, for instance, not only are excellent sources of vegetable protein, they are practically fat-free and terrific sources of complex carbohydrates.

Change your protein habits

One mistake many people make is to eat most of their day's protein at dinner. You'll feel better if you eat protein earlier,

45

because it will stabilize your blood sugar throughout the day.

In other words, instead of eating meat, chicken, or fish only at dinnertime, consider starting the day with a small portion of leftovers from last night's supper. Be sure to include another small helping of additional protein at lunch and dinner.

For maximum nutrition, eat a variety of protein sources. If you're a vegetarian, have as much variety as possible—eggs and dairy products, grains, legumes, and nuts—every day, to make sure you're getting complete protein.

One of the best sources of protein is red meat. This includes beef, pork, veal, lamb, and mutton. They are important sources of iron and zinc, two nutrients Americans have trouble getting in sufficient amounts. But because red meat is high in fat, you'll have to limit your servings to 5 ounces, once or twice a week.

FAT-BURNING FOOD TIP #8

- -

Plan to eat one or two dinners of lean red meat weekly, another one or two dinners featuring chicken, another one or two of fish, and at least one vegetarian dinner a week, preferably two.

Meat today is much leaner, especially if you trim off excess fat and cook it in lower-fat ways (you'll learn more about food preparation in the next chapter). Many lean cuts of beef and pork have less fat per serving than fatty fish like trout and salmon.

One meat you might consider substituting for beef is pork, which can be almost as low in fat as chicken in terms of its content of total and saturated fat.

FAT-BURNING FOOD TIP #9

Never eat more than 5 ounces of animal protein in a day.

Dairy Dilemma: Getting Calcium Without the Fat

Dairy foods provide many vital nutrients, including protein, vitamin A, riboflavin, niacin, vitamin B-12, and folacin. Their most significant nutrient, however, is calcium and, in fortified milk, vitamin D.

You need calcium, which is stored in your bones, for muscles, nerves, blood, and cell membrane functioning. If you don't eat enough of it, your body will take calcium from your bones, eventually making them so porous that you could develop osteoporosis. Women especially must ensure there is sufficient calcium in their diets. After menopause, they must have a good source of calcium for prevention of osteoporosis.

FAT-BURNING FOOD TIP #10

Avoid whole milk and hard cheese.

PERCENTAGE OF CALORIES FROM FAT IN COMMON DAIRY FOODS

Dairy food	Calories	Percentage of calories from fat
Whole milk, 1 cup	150	49%
2% milk, 1 cup	121	35%
1% milk, 1 cup	102	22%
Skim (nonfat) milk, 1 cup	86	5%
Light cheddar cheese, 1 oz. (a slice)	90	56%
Mozzarella cheese, 1 oz. (a slice)	70	64%
Parmesan cheese, 1 oz.	129	59%
Fat-free cheddar cheese, 1 oz.	40	—
Fat-free mozzarella cheese, 1 oz.	40	—
1% cottage cheese, 4 oz. ($^1/_2$ cup)	90	10%
Fat-free process cheese spread, 1 oz.	30	—

The trouble is, the most common sources of whole milk and hard cheese are very high in fat.

Skim milk is just as nutritious as whole milk, and has a fraction of the fat. If you switch from drinking two glasses of whole milk a day to two glasses of skim milk, you'll save yourself 18 grams of fat. You can drink up to two glasses of skim milk a day, or the equivalent amount of low-fat yogurt or cottage cheese. Eat low-fat cheese products in moderation.

It's advisable to eat as little hard cheese as possible on this program, and only low-fat varieties.

Many people, particularly African-Americans and those

Christine Timmons:
Too Busy to Diet

CHRISTINE IS A SUCCESSFUL BUSINESSWOMAN. Her work takes her into the highest social circles, not only in her native New York, but all over the world. Unfortunately, it also takes her into the world's best restaurants, and keeps her so busy that exercise during the day is out of the question. Nonetheless, once she noticed that she was 20 pounds overweight, she began to fear that the "price" of those excess pounds could be her next big promotion.

Her "diet" of choice was 600-calorie-a-day starvation, even though constant hunger cravings made her late-night business dealings a real challenge. Usually she'd lose five pounds the first week and two pounds the second week, but after that, the pounds would start creeping back again.

She'd wait a month or two, then try again. Each time a new diet came out, she was the first on the bandwagon, all to no avail.

Then she decided to do one thing and one thing only: cut out fat, whenever possible. She started by eliminating the butter on her toast in the morning and on her sandwiches at lunch, as well as cake for desserts. That one change alone enabled Christine to lose four pounds within a month.

Then she got even more serious. Instead of steak dinners, she started ordering broiled fish. She began to enjoy the taste of foods without sauces over them, and made it a point of ordering salad, with diet dressing, for at least one meal daily.

Another six pounds dropped off within a month, and Christine realized that most days she could probably add in a morning walk, if she set her alarm to ring a half-hour earlier.

Two months later, Christine fits into her best dress-for-success wardrobe. And she hasn't been hungry since!

from Mediterranean areas, are not able to drink milk at all because they are "lactose-intolerant." Their systems cannot handle the natural sugar in milk. Lactose-intolerant people can get the calcium they need by using an over-the-counter product that neutralizes the lactose in milk.

Fortunately, dairy products require no preparation: for a thirst-quenching, energizing snack, just grab a glass and pour out milk, spoon yogurt into a bowl, or nibble on a slice of low-fat cheese.

Here are a few tips to help you incorporate low-fat dairy products into your diet:

➤ Make drinks or soups using skim milk.

➤ Add a dollop of low-fat yogurt to cold soups.

➤ Replace oil or mayonnaise with low-fat yogurt in a dip for fruits and vegetables, or as a base for salad dressings.

➤ Combine low-fat grated cheeses with wheat germ or whole-wheat bread crumbs as toppings for casseroles.

➤ Spread your morning toast with fat-free cream cheese instead of butter.

Understanding Food Labels

When you buy packaged food, read the label to look for fat and fiber content. The new nutrition labels that began appearing in 1994 (see sample label) show the number of calories per serving. You'll also learn how much fat, cholesterol, sodium, carbohydrates, and protein the food contains, by weight and percentage.

The new labels not only indicate the total calories in food, but the amount of calories from fat. They also list the grams of fat per serving and provide a Daily Value (% Daily Value) for that fat. This is the percentage of daily fat intake each serving contains. Always choose the product that has the lowest possible % Daily Value (DV) of fat.

But don't let a low DV figure fool you; it's only the amount considered "healthy" if you're on a 2,000-calorie-a-day diet and eating 65 grams of fat per day. As the label itself indicates, your daily values may be higher or lower, depending on your calorie needs. Sixty-five grams of fat per day on a 2,000-calorie diet means you'll eat 30 percent fat from calories, the very upper limit we recommend for weight loss.

Remember too, that if you eat twice as much as the suggested serving size, you're also eating twice of everything in that food, including the fat.

On this program, the food should be no more than 20 to 30 percent fat, preferably closer to 20 percent. To ensure this is the case, perform the following calculation based on label information:

A. Calories from fat: _____
B. Total calories: _____
C. To determine the percentage of food composed of fat, divide the total calories from fat (A) by the total calories (B), then multiply by 100: _____

THE NEW FOOD LABEL AT A GLANCE

Nutrition Facts

Serving Size 1 cup (228g)
Servings Per Container 2

Amount Per Serving

Calories 260   Calories from Fat 120

	% Daily Value*
Total Fat 13g	**20**%
Saturated Fat 5g	**25**%
Cholesterol 30mg	**10**%
Sodium 660mg	**28**%
Total Carbohydrate 31g	**10**%
Dietary Fiber 0g	**0**%
Sugars 5g	
Protein 5g	

Vitamin A 4%	•	Vitamin C 2%
Calcium 15%	•	Iron 4%

* Percent Daily Values are based on a 2,000
calorie diet. Your daily values may be higher
or lower depending on your calorie needs:

	Calories:	2,000	2,500
Total Fat	Less than	65g	80g
Sat Fat	Less than	20g	25g
Cholesterol	Less than	300mg	300mg
Sodium	Less than	2,400mg	2,400mg
Total Carbohydrate		300g	375g
Dietary Fiber		25g	30g

Calories per gram:
Fat 9 • Carbohydrate 4 • Protein 4

Source: Food and Drug Administration, 1994

Here's an example, based on information from the food label on page 52.

A. Calories from fat: 120
B. Total calories: 260
C. Percentage of food composed of fat:
$(\underline{120} \div \underline{260}) \times 100 = 46\%$.
   A   B

The label also shows the ingredients in the food, listed in order of their proportion by weight. A product that lists apples before sugar contains more apples by weight than sugar.

Look for the total fat content on the label. It will tell you how many grams there are of polyunsaturates, monounsaturates, saturates, cholesterol, and trans fatty acids. Because you want to restrict your purchases to products with little or no fats in them, look for—and avoid—foods that contain items such as oil, shortening, butter, chocolate or milk chocolate, cocoa butter, cream, egg and egg-yolk solids, glycerolesters, lard, mono- or diglycerides, suet, or whole milk solids.

To avoid unnecessary sugars in your diet, look for—and avoid—foods that contain the following, especially if one appears first, or if several are listed:

Corn syrup	Gluco-fructose	Maple syrup
Dextrose	Glucose	Molasses
Fructose	Honey	Sucrose
Fruit juice	Lactose	Sugar
concentrate	Maltose	Syrup

The art of label reading

New USDA food label regulations have standardized the application of certain terms used by food manufacturers on products. Here's what those terms mean to you:

If it says **fat-free, without fat, no fat,** or **zero fat,** the food has fewer than 0.5 grams of fat per serving.

If it says **calorie-free, without calories, no calories,** or **zero calories,** the food has fewer than 5 calories per serving.

In general, **low** means the same as **little, few,** and **low source of. Low-fat** means 3 grams of fat (or less) per serving. **Low calorie** means 40 calories or less per serving. **Low cholesterol** means 20 milligrams or less, and 2 grams or less of saturated fat per serving. **Low saturated fat** means 1 gram or less per serving.

Lean means fewer than 10 grams of fat, 4 grams of saturated fat, and 95 milligrams of cholesterol per serving and per 100 grams. If the serving size is relatively small, these foods may still contain a relatively high percentage of fat calories per serving.

Extra-lean means fewer than 10 grams of fat, 2 grams of saturated fat, and 95 milligrams of cholesterol per serving and per 100 grams.

Less or **fewer** means the food contains 25 percent less of a nutrient or of calories than a comparative product. The label may say, for example, that pretzels have 25 percent less fat than potato chips.

Reduced means the product contains at least 25 percent less of a nutrient or of calories than the regular product. This claim can't be made if the regular food already meets the requirement for being **low** in fat, calories, or cholesterol.

Percent fat-free should provide an accurate description of the amount of fat present in a low-fat or fat-free product. If a food contains 5 grams of fat per 100 grams, for instance, the label would say 95 percent fat-free.

Don't be fooled by labels such as **light** or **lite**. These words may refer to color, texture, flavor, alcohol content, sodium content, or fat content. **Light** soy sauce, for instance, could be low in sodium. **Light** olive oil could be light in color; it's still 100 percent fat. If the label **light** or **lite** does refer to fat content, this means the food has one-third fewer calories, or no more than half the fat, of the higher-calorie, higher-fat version.

Likewise, the label **cholesterol-free** can be deceptive. It means the food has no more than 2 milligrams of dietary cholesterol and 2 grams (or less) of saturated fat per serving. The product could still contain unsaturated or some saturated fats. Vegetable oils, for instance, are cholesterol-free, but they are almost entirely unsaturated fat.

Even a label like **95% fat-free** could be deceptive, because it may refer to the percentage fat-free by weight, not the percentage fat-free by calories. Turkey ham, for instance, which is advertised as "95% fat-free," still provides more than half its calories from fat.

Dairy products must contain between 0.5 and 2 percent milk fat to be labelled **low-fat. Low-fat** meat can be no more than 10 percent fat by weight.

The truth about health claims

New food labels can carry claims about the relationship between nutrients and diseases. However, they can only suggest the relationship by using words such as "may" or "might." They also imply that other factors can play a role in causing disease.

Here's a guide to health claims you may find on labels:

Osteoporosis prevention and calcium intake. The label can point out that people who need calcium most for prevention of osteoporosis include teens and young adult white and Asian women. Calcium-rich foods that claim to prevent or delay the onset of osteoporosis must contain 20 percent or more of the Daily Value for calcium, have a calcium content equal to or greater than its phosphorous content, and contain a form of calcium our bodies can easily absorb and use. If the food has 40 percent or more of the Daily Value for calcium, the label must further state that a total dietary intake greater than 200 percent of the Daily Value has no further known benefit.

Cancer prevention and fat intake. Only **low fat** foods or **extra lean** fish and game meats may make this claim.

Cancer prevention and eating fiber-containing grain products, fruits, and vegetables. Food must be or must contain a grain product, fruit, or vegetable, be a good source of dietary fiber (without fortification), and be **low fat.**

Cancer prevention and eating fruits and vegetables. The fruits must be **low fat** and a **good source** (without fortification) of dietary fiber and/or vitamins A or C.

Coronary heart disease prevention and eating foods low in saturated fat and cholesterol intake. These foods also meet the criteria for **low saturated fat, low cholesterol, low fat,** or, if fish and game meats, **extra lean.**

Coronary heart disease prevention and eating fiber-con-

Jeffrey Binley:
Milk Shake Man

IN HIS YOUNGER DAYS, when Jeff was into weightlifting, football, and other energetic pursuits, he quaffed a quart of milk a day. He thought he needed that much milk to keep his bones strong.

By the time he entered his forties, Jeff's athletic career was long behind him, but not his fondness for dairy products. He still downed that same quart of milk daily, but also enjoyed milk shakes, sour cream, and lots of cheese. He was 30 pounds overweight when he had his first heart attack.

His doctor prescribed a daily walk and a low-fat diet as part of his recovery process. He explained to Jeff that all the dairy products he was consuming were high in saturated fat—the worst possible kind of fat for people with heart conditions. Jeff learned that a low-fat diet can make fatty deposits in coronary arteries start to shrink, especially if the sufferer also quits smoking, exercises sensibly, and keeps stress under control.

His doctor also pointed out that being overweight was exactly the kind of strain Jeff's body didn't need: his heart had to pump blood through all the extra arteries his body had grown to feed his fat deposits.

Jeff decided to replace the whole milk he'd been drinking with skim milk. He started whirling low-fat yogurt and fruit in the blender to replace the milk shakes of old. He discovered that thickened low-fat yogurt was practically indistinguishable from sour cream on top of baked potatoes and in chicken stroganoff dishes. And he learned to love beans, instead of cheese, on toast.

Because his work was so high-stress, Jeff also decided to take up yoga on his lunch hours. The stretching and relaxing poses helped keep him calm and collected, and away from double martinis.

Today he's trim, energetic, and—best of all—healthy.

taining grain products, fruits, and vegetables. Aside from containing grain products, fruits, and vegetables, the food has to meet the criteria for **low saturated fat, low cholesterol, and low fat,** and contain (without fortification) at least 0.6 grams of soluble fiber per serving.

Hypertension (high blood pressure) control and eating a low-sodium diet. The food must be **low sodium.**

Active Benefits: Get a Move On!

There's one simple fact that you need to know about exercise. **Regular activity keeps your basal metabolic rate high enough to burn off body fat.** Even hours after activity, your basal metabolic rate remains raised.

As you have learned, the diets you might have followed in the past encouraged your body to call on its "hunger troops" to maintain the *status quo,* thinking it is "fighting for survival." As the hunger continued and your body thought it was starving, it decreased its metabolic rate in order to conserve energy. That's where exercise comes in: it increases your metabolic rate to keep those pounds rolling off.

Exercise also encourages your body to burn fat stores instead of carbohydrate stores or muscle. Studies have shown that weight loss from dieting alone leads to a loss of about 75 percent fat and 25 percent muscle. When physical activity is added, muscle loss can be reduced to 5 percent.

And, of course, exercise burns off calories. If you perform 500 calories of exercise a week, you'll lose 4 to 5 pounds within a year even on your present diet—weight you wouldn't have lost without that activity. The more active you are, the more calories you can consume and still lose or maintain your weight.

Furthermore, physical activity changes your body composition by building muscle and reducing fat. It's in your interest to keep your muscle mass up and the amount of fat in your body down. Muscle requires more energy to sustain itself than fat stores. So the more muscle you have in your body, the easier it is to stay slim. An increase in your musculature increases your daily caloric burn-off, even when you're not exercising, because muscle requires more energy to maintain than fat.

As you get older, some of your muscle will be replaced by fat, a natural part of the aging process. This means it's even more important to keep active in order to prevent or slow down the replacement of muscle by fat. Muscle weighs more than fat and occupies less space.

Furthermore, exercise keeps food moving along quickly through your digestive tract, which means foods that might otherwise add calories to your body may not be fully-absorbed.

Not insignificantly, exercise also makes you feel more energetic and good about yourself and your eating program. You'll sleep better, cope with stress better, deal with the ups and downs of life more calmly. This vitality can only help you in the long run.

What type of exercise is best for weight loss? Believe it or not, you don't have to "go for the burn" to maximize fat-burning potential. In fact, if you work too hard at your workout, your body could stop drawing on your fat stores for food and start depending on your carbohydrate supplies.

That's why an activity like walking is the absolutely best form of exercise. The idea is to decrease the intensity of a workout and increase the amount of time you spend at moderate activity. In the next chapter, you'll learn about specific activities that can keep weight rolling off.

What About My "Bad Genes"?

Most overweight people blame their problem on bad genes or bad eating habits when they were growing up. They've got a point.

If one of your parents is overweight, the likelihood of your being overweight is 40 to 50 percent. If both your parents are overweight, the likelihood jumps to 70 to 80 percent. It's hard to determine whether this happens because of heredity or the family environment. The chances of being overweight when you come from a family that had a weekend ritual of going for walks is certainly lower than in one whose favored activity is eating out.

Dr. Albert Sunkard, obesity specialist at the University of Pennsylvania, studied hundreds of adopted people in Denmark. He discovered there was no relationship between how overweight adoptees were, compared to their adoptive parents. But there was considerable correlation between overweight and natural parents. In other words, children of heavy parents who were adopted by thin folks still tended to end up overweight. Here is more confirmation that heredity strongly influences your adult body shape.

Nonetheless, **no matter what your gene pool, no matter how you were brought up, you can still lose weight!**

Although your genes—or your childhood home environment—may determine your basal metabolic rate and how

---

EXERCISE AND CALORIE EXPENDITURE

Activity	Calories expended per hour[1]	
	Man[2]	Woman[2]
Sitting quietly	100	80
Standing quietly	120	95
Light activity: Cleaning house Office work Playing baseball Playing golf	300	240
Moderate activity: Walking briskly (3.5 mph) Gardening Cycling (5.5 mph) Dancing Playing basketball	460	370
Strenuous activity: Jogging (9 min./mile) Playing football Swimming	730	580
Very strenuous activity: Running (7 min./mile) Racquetball Skiing	920	740

[1]May vary depending on environmental conditions. [2]Healthy man, 175 lbs; healthy woman, 140 lbs. Source: McArdle, et al., Exercise Physiology, 1986.

---

much fat you carry and where, this program will help you develop a healthy attitude towards food and will certainly help you lose weight if you have a genetic predisposition to amass body fat. This program is an effective combatant to heredity. It will work for anyone.

Furthermore, if you believe a hormonal problem accounts for your figure size, or that your metabolism is the problem, you should have a doctor examine you. But almost certainly, you'll find out this program will take off those pounds.

Once you get used to the taste of fresh foods prepared without fatty sauces—and once you start making food selections from our list of 30 fat-burning foods—you'll quickly get rid of your taste for grease.

Best of all, if you raise your children in an environment where they eat lots of vegetables and little meat, and drink 1 percent milk instead of whole milk, there's a good chance they can remain slender when they get older, despite their genetic heritage.

That's My Cue!

There are two different kinds of "cues," or appetite stimulators, that eaters respond to: internal or external.

Internally-cued eaters are people who eat when their bodies need food. They eat in response to "hunger" signals the body sends, such as a grumbling tummy.

Unfortunately, many overweight people are *externally-cued eaters,* or ECEs (pronounced "Eeks," as in "Eeks! I want to eat!"). ECEs tend to eat in response to cues from the world around them. Their situation, rather than their body's needs, frequently "tells" ECEs to consume food, whether or not they're hungry. Externally-cued eaters will have lunch at the stroke of noon, for example, instead of waiting until they're hungry. They'll eat "because it's there," or in response to a hundred other distractions, such as depression, social anxiety at a party, even the presence of other people.

A study at Georgia State University, for instance, found that when six or more people ate together in a group, their food intake soared by 76 percent! Even when two people ate together, their food intake was 28 percent greater than when they ate alone. (Not surprisingly, this effect is particularly noticeable at dessert time.)

If you're an externally-cued eater, you can try alternative activities to overeating. Many of these are provided for you in the next chapter.

There's no point in starting a diet if you don't feel good about yourself. Although you'll probably like yourself better once you've lost weight, you need self-esteem to help you stick to any self-improvement program. At first, you may need lots of support from friends, or even professional help, in order to stick to this program. If you're a compulsive eater, Overeaters Anonymous has helped thousands of participants break their food addictions. There's probably a chapter near you!

The fact is, psychological disturbances are more likely to be caused by being overweight than by compulsive overeating. You'll find yourself more emotionally healthy after you've lost weight.

Fat-Burning Basics

You've now learned the eleven basic rules of this amazing new weight-loss program:

➤ Eat as much as you want of the 30 amazing fat-burning foods.

➤ Enjoy just about as much complex carbohydrate foods as you need in order to feel full. These foods must provide at least 65 percent of your daily calories.

➤ Aim to eat at least 30 to 40 grams of fiber every day. To keep your fiber level up, read the label of packaged foods, and always buy the higher-fiber product (it's also usually the lower-fat item).

➤ Consume 20 to 30 percent of your total daily calories as fat. To keep life simple, avoid fat whenever possible. For health reasons, you should keep your intake of saturated fats (the "solid" type found in animal fat, butters, cheeses, "hydrogenated" margarine, and tropical vegetable oils) at or below 10 percent of your daily calorie intake.

➤ Eat a maximum of 10 to 15 percent of your daily calories in animal protein.

➤ Stick to fewer than 5 ounces of animal protein daily, and no more than two dinners of lean red meat weekly.

➤ Eat at least one vegetarian dinner a week, preferably two.

➤ Eat as little hard cheese as possible, and low-fat varieties in moderation.

➤ Drink up to two glasses of skim milk a day, or the equivalent amount of low-fat yogurt or cottage cheese.

➤ Enjoy regular activity, which will keep your metabolism high enough to burn off body fat.

CHAPTER 2

STEP-BY-STEP TO A SLIMMER YOU

YOU'VE NOW LEARNED EVERYTHING you need to successfully lose weight. On a day-to-day basis, however, temptation in the form of your old habits is your biggest obstacle to permanent weight loss.

Here are some suggestions that will *guarantee* diet success!

1. Slow and steady wins the diet race. As you've already learned, losing too much weight too quickly is a sign that you're starving yourself. Such dieting makes your body hang on to every bit of body fat it can. A 1- or 2-pounds-a-week loss will ensure that you lose weight, keep it off, and stay healthy.

2. Weigh yourself once a week—or less. Your weight will fluctuate on a daily basis, and this may discourage you when, in fact, you're losing weight on a weekly or monthly basis.

3. Take the program one day at a time, but make a long-term commitment to successfully lose your excess weight. You'll enjoy this program and feel proud of your decision to become a new, healthy you. **You can do it!**

4. Do it for yourself—not to make your husband or wife happy, get a new job, or impress your former classmates at your high school reunion.

5. Variety is important. Remember the grapefruit-only diet? No one can live like that for long—and you deserve better. The fat-burning foods on this plan will provide you with hundreds of exciting meal combinations.

6. If the support of others trying to lose weight will help you, join a group like Overeaters Anonymous, or form your own group.

7. Be kind to yourself. The night you go on a chocolate cake binge is not the end of the world. It's also not the end of this program. The very next day, pick yourself up again and renew your commitment.

8. Experiment to discover the meal pattern that works for you. If you're sure of your pattern, eat a good breakfast. Then, eat just enough to satisfy your appetite for the other two meals of the day, keeping track of your food intake. Monitor your resulting hunger. If you find dinner is your hungry time, plan to eat a little extra at lunch and an afternoon snack. You may discover that you're hungry in the morning, but satisfied with a snack for dinner. Alternatively, you may find that you wake up with no appetite at all, but crave food before bedtime.

Replace Old Habits With Fat-Burning Activities

Because new habits extend well beyond the dinner table, it's often helpful to observe which situations trigger your bad overeating ways, and then substitute other behaviors.

Consider keeping a food diary for a week or two. Record every bit of food you eat, the amount, the time of day, the place, who you were with at the time, what you were doing, how you were feeling, and what might have made you eat (aside from hunger).

You'll learn a lot about your own special "triggers" for overeating. You may discover that cookie binges almost always follow a fight with your children. Or that you never eat when you're alone. Or that you tend to gulp down leftovers, rather than toss them into the garbage.

Make a point of discovering one of your "triggers" and working on *only* that problem. After a month, see if you can discover another trigger, and tackle that one. (If you try to change everything at once, you may get discouraged and give up.) By taking on one trigger a month, you'll have changed your eating habits for the better within a year!

To get you started, here are just a few "alternative behavior" suggestions for overeating:

➤ Force yourself to eat regular meals and then, when the urge to snack hits, go for a walk, play tennis, or write an angry entry in your diary. Do anything but eat to handle your stress (as long as it's legal and doesn't hurt anyone). "Train" yourself to eat from hunger, not from other factors.

➤ Instead of snacking while you watch TV, start crocheting, basketweaving, sketching, doodling, or embroidering—any activity that'll keep your hands busy.

➤ Walk the dog after dinner, instead of reading that novel accompanied by a bag of potato chips.

➤ Put leftovers away immediately after mealtime. You don't need them tempting you when you're not hungry. Forget about "clean plate" clubs and starving children in other countries.

➤ Alternatively, feed leftovers to the dog or actually throw them out. That makes a lot more sense than using yourself as a human garbage can, doesn't it?

➤ If you can't resist eating leftovers "just to get rid of them," talk your spouse or children into clearing the table.

➤ Treat yourself to flowers, a novel, a new dress, or tickets to a baseball game instead of a box of cookies.

➤ Figure out ways that do not involve food to show your children and spouse that you love them. Your children would probably enjoy a game of frisbee with you more than your home-baked cookies.

➤ Prepare your low-fat snacks ahead of time, so you don't find yourself getting hungry with no fat-burning foods to eat in the house.

➤ Ask your kids to make their own snacks, or make them yourself at mealtime and package them for later snacking.

➤ Stay clear of the cafeteria or junk machines at work if they offer nothing healthy to eat. Bring your own lunch to work, or find a restaurant that serves fat-burning foods.

➤ If your kids like to eat high-fat cookies, make sure you buy them varieties you don't like.

➤ Change the route of your daily walk if it takes you past an inviting bakery or restaurant.

Healthy Mealtime Tricks to Stave Off Temptation

You've spent a long time developing the poor eating habits that made you overweight. Be patient with yourself as you develop healthy new eating habits at mealtime; soon you'll lose your taste for unhealthy foods. But in the meantime . . .

DO

➤ Eat enough to satisfy yourself, and then stop.

➤ Put less food than you're used to on your fork or spoon, chew it thoroughly, and put your fork down between bites. It takes at least 20 minutes for your brain to tell your stomach it's full, so eat slowly.

➤ Serve your food on a smaller plate than you're accustomed to. You may find the smaller portions will fill you up.

➤ Set your table properly, and eat only at the kitchen table. Don't watch TV or read, even if you eat alone. This will reduce the number of locations you associate with eating.

➤ Concentrate on your meal. Inhale it (with your nose!), enjoy the look of it, feel its texture in your mouth, eat it slowly.

➤ Serve from the stove or countertop, not from a serving platter loaded with food you don't need.

➤ Take only one helping, and leave the table as soon as your hunger is satisfied.

DON'T

➤ Skip meals. Overweight people typically skip breakfast, eat a modest lunch and a generous dinner, and then snack all night long. Always start your day with breakfast, and eat according to your body's natural hunger patterns throughout the day.

➤ Eat when you're not hungry.

➤ Eat foods you really don't want to eat out of politeness or obligation.

➤ Eat because you're bored, upset, depressed, anxious, or otherwise emotional.

➤ Eat because you're afraid you might be hungry later.

➤ Put more on your plate than you want to eat at that meal.

Diet-Proofing Your Home

One way to ensure you will not return to your unhealthy eating habits is to get rid of those "fat-making" foods. Toss out food that's not good for you! Then, replace the food that's bad for your waistline with substitutes.

➤ Toss out your stash of chocolates, hard candies, packaged fruit snacks, cookies, cakes, danishes, even granola bars. Ditto for regular mayonnaise, sour cream, regular salad dressings, and guacamole.

➤ Although you can enjoy limited quantities of dairy products, discard your whole milk, dairy creamer, whipped cream, regular cheese, and regular yogurt.

➤ Processed meats are a no-no. That includes bacon, bologna, corned beef, hot dogs, liverwurst, pastrami, pepperoni, salami, and sausage.

➤ Say goodbye forever to regular ground beef, chicken wings and backs, high-fat cuts of beef or pork, creamy soups, gravies made with drippings, pastry, cake or ice cream, chips, and cheese puffs.

➤ Say hello to all the fat-burning alternatives that are just as tasty, just as filling, and are guaranteed to make you lose weight.

If other people in your life (like your slender spouse or your teenager) must keep food in the house that's not good for you, rearrange your fridge and cupboard to keep them out of sight. You can also store tempting foods in containers you can't see through.

Shopping for Success

The main thing you'll want to do, of course, is to stock up on the 30 fabulous fat-burning foods that will enable you to lose weight. You'll want lots of these foods around the house so you can grab a snack or create a filling meal without having to fight temptation.

Buy a variety of fruits and vegetables and eat them raw as often as possible. If you're short on time, buy cleaned and chopped vegetables from your supermarket's salad bar. You'll spend a little more, but you'll cut down on time-consuming food preparation.

As for meeting protein requirements, try these tips:

➤ Buy enough fish or white meat of poultry to make them your protein source. After all, aside from one or two meals a week, you will be replacing red meat with the white meat of chicken or turkey, fish, or vegetable proteins.

➤ Buy more modest portions of meat than you used to. You don't need more than 5 ounces of animal protein a day.

➤ Buy the leanest cuts of meat available. Cuts from a young animal, such as veal, or from the parts of an animal that are more muscular, such as round or foreshank, are leaner than cuts from the loin area and breast.

➤ Ask your butcher to grind sirloin, or buy ground turkey or chicken breast instead.

➤ Choose ground chicken or turkey over higher-fat ground beef, veal, or pork, but only if the meat has been ground without the skin. The label should specifically say "breast meat."

➤ Choose chicken over pork. A cut of trimmed pork has one-third more fat than skinless chicken and twice as much fat as skinless turkey.

➤ Plan to replace animal proteins with vegetable proteins for at least one meal a week—preferably two. Foods such as tofu, soybeans, lentils, chick peas, and beans are low in fat, less expensive than meat, yet just as tasty, and rich in fiber and nutrients.

Poultry picks

In general, choose turkey over chicken, and white meat over dark meat. Remove the skin, which is all fat, before you indulge.

What's the matter with chicken? It has one-and-a-half times more fat than turkey! Similarly, breast meat is considerably lower in fat than dark meat. Chicken breast (without skin) has approximately 23 percent of its calories from fat, while dark meat (without skin) has about 43 percent of its calories from fat. Chicken thigh, in contrast, is as high in fat as many red meats. In fact, 47 percent of its calories come from fat, which makes it fattier than grade round steak, sirloin, or chuck arm pot roast. It also has nearly as much fat content as pork tender-loin, top loin, or the rump of a ham leg—assuming you trim every bit of fat off the red meats. As for chicken wings, they're 36 percent fat, even when roasted; the figure jumps to 39 percent fat when fried.

FATS AND CHOLESTEROL IN COOKED POULTRY

Type	Percent of fat by weight	Percent of calories from fat
Turkey, light meat (roasted)		
without skin	3	19
with skin	8	38
Turkey, dark meat (roasted)		
without skin	7	35
with skin	12	47
Chicken, light meat (roasted)		
without skin	5	23
with skin	11	44
Chicken, dark meat (roasted)		
without skin	10	43
with skin	16	56

Source: U.S. Department of Agriculture Handbook No. 8-5

Not all turkeys, however, are created equal. Avoid self-basting or deep-basted turkey. As you'll see from the label, it has been injected with butter, oil, or turkey broth. Likewise, prestuffed birds are a no-no; the stuffing is generally high-fat.

The best of beef

Even after you trim all visible fat, beef is still relatively high in fat compared to your fat-burning foods. You may eat up to 5 ounces (6 ounces raw) of the following cuts once or twice a week. (That's a piece of meat about the size of your hand.)

Choose From the Leanest Cuts of Beef
(Choice Grade)

Top round (29% fat)
Eye of round steak (30% fat)
Round tip (sirloin tip, tip steak, or tip roast) (36% fat)
Top sirloin steak (36% fat)
Top loin (New York steak, strip steak) (40% fat)
Tenderloin (filet mignon, chateaubriand) (38% fat)

Avoid the Fattiest Cuts of Beef

Chuck blade roast (72% fat)
Flank steak (51% fat if lean; up to 58% if lean and fat)
Ribs (75% fat)
Brisket (48% if whole and lean; 75% if lean and fat-braised)
Porterhouse steak (44 to 64% fat)
T-bone (68% fat)
Tongue (66% if simmered; 98% if medium-fat and braised)

At the supermarket, choose meat with the least amount of "marbling." The higher the concentration of marbling, the more fat it contains.

Be careful when purchasing ground meat. Regular ground beef can be 30 percent fat from calories. Switch to lean ground meat and the percentage drops to 17 percent fat from calories.

Pork possibilities

Pork has received bad press at times, but it can be as low in fat as chicken if you select carefully, trim visible fat, and avoid frying it.

Choose From the Leanest Cuts of Pork

Center loin pork chops (26% fat)
Center loin pork roast (26% fat)
Tenderloin (26% fat)

Avoid the Fattiest Cuts of Pork

Loin blade steaks (50% fat)
Ribs (54% fat)
Top loin (36% fat)
Shoulder blade steaks (51% fat)
Bacon (40 to 90% fat)

Lean on lamb

When selecting and preparing lamb, look out for marbling, trim the fat, and avoid frying. Ribs and chops are especially

Shopping Tips

TRY THESE GROCERY SHOPPING suggestions to help you lose weight and win.

➤ Make a rough menu for the week and shop from that list, checking for the foods you need that are not already on hand.

➤ Divide your shopping list into the same areas as the grocery store departments.

➤ Shop alone so you can get in and out of the store quickly.

➤ Do your grocery shopping after mealtime, not before. Never shop on an empty stomach.

➤ Shop strictly from your shopping list, and never buy anything that is not on your list.

➤ Read all labels on the foods you buy to determine if they have any hidden sugars. Sugars include corn syrup, dextrose, fructose, gluco-fructose, glucose, honey, maple syrup, molasses, maltose, and sucrose.

➤ Also read all labels to ensure that you are avoiding hidden fats. Fat information on the label will include grams of total fat per serving, as well as the amount that is saturated fat and cholesterol. The list of fats in the ingredients include any oil or shortening, butter, chocolate or milk chocolate, cocoa butter, cream, egg and egg-yolk solids, glycerolesters, lard, mono- or diglycerides, suet, and whole milk solids.

➤ Whenever possible (for example, with foods such as cereal and bread), buy the higher-fiber product; it's listed on the label as "dietary fiber."

high in fat. You should also avoid lamb breast. Your best bets are shanks (44 percent fat) and the sirloin portion of the leg (39 percent fat).

Focus on fish

In general, fish is a good low-fat alternative to red meat and even poultry. Shellfish, however, are high in dietary cholesterol, which may be bad for your heart. Avoid marinated fish or those canned in oil.

Healthy Hardware

Aside from the new foods you'll be eating, it's wise to stock up on the basic equipment you'll need in order to prepare these foods. You'll need non-stick frying pans, cookie sheets, loaf pans, casserole dishes, and baking dishes. Plastic utensils and a plastic scrubber are necessary in order to prevent scratching.

A good blender, food processor, or food-chopper is a time-saver when making delicious dressings and chopping up vegetables and fruit.

If your budget permits, a microwave oven is not only a time-saver, but will enable you to create low-fat meals in minutes.

Substitute, Don't Sacrifice

If you really crave the taste of fat in your food, there's no reason why you can't use one of the FDA-approved fat substitutes now available on the market. They have no nutritional value, of

SHOPPING ALTERNATIVES

Instead of	Buy
Whole milk, dairy creamer	Skim milk
Regular cheese	Low-fat cheese
Regular yogurt	Low-fat yogurt
Pork, beef, ham, or cold cuts	Turkey, chicken, fish
Processed meats (such as bacon, bologna, corned beef, hot dogs, salami, sausage)	Sliced chicken, turkey, low-fat meat substute
Ground beef	Ground trimmed cuts of beef
Your usual cuts of beef and pork	Top round steak, sirloin steak, eye of round, pork tenderloin
Your usual cuts of pork, bacon	Pork tenderloin
Creamy soups, gravies made with drippings	Clear soups and broths
Pastry, cake, or ice cream	Fruit
Eggs	Egg whites or low-fat egg substitutes
Chips, cheese puffs	Air-popped popcorn, low-fat pretzels
Chicken wings and backs	Turkey breast, chicken breast

course, but they're not bad for you.

Olestra, an experimental fat substitute, tastes, feels, and acts like fat. Your body doesn't have enzymes to break it down, so you can eat as much of this substitute as you want and it will be eliminated. According to one study, replacing fat with Olestra not only makes people's fat intake go down, but also makes their carbohydrate intake go up. *Simplesse* is also harmless, but you can't cook with it and it's only available in a few products.

As you learned in the last chapter, you can enjoy the occasional treat like sugary candy, which is made of refined and/or processed sugars, and not worry about gaining weight. The trouble is, such treats not only damage your teeth, they have no nutritional value. Sugar alone makes your blood glucose level go up very fast and drop just as quickly, leaving you as hungry as before. Furthermore, dietary sugar is usually accompanied by plenty of fat. You must avoid high-fat sugary treats, such as cakes, pies, and chocolate bars.

Substitute diet soft drinks for sugary ones, and use NutraSweet or other sugar substitutes when possible. Artificial sweeteners, such as NutraSweet and saccharine, won't harm you unless you suffer from phenylketonuria, a relatively rare disease.

Kill Those Caffeine Cravings!

Strictly speaking, caffeine is not a food, but a chemical found in coffee, tea, chocolate, soda, and many drugs. It acts as a stimulant, increasing alertness and raising blood pressure. In excess amounts, caffeine may cause heartburn or indigestion, increase the rate of calcium loss from bone (a serious side-effect if you're suffering from osteoporosis), and put you at risk for cardiovascular disease. Caffeine can also cause premature or irregular heartbeats. You should avoid caffeine if you have any heart problems, especially heart rhythm irregularities.

If you have no such health problems, there's no reason to avoid coffee, tea, and other drinks that have moderate amounts of caffeine in them. Caffeine has no calories. It may even start a complex hormonal reaction that accelerates your body's release of fat from its fat stores. But caffeine would be unlikely to help you lose weight because the fat would still be in your body.

Thirst-Quenching News

Drinking water can be good for your waistline! Drinking up to eight 8-ounce glasses daily helps to flush out your system and keeps tummy-rumbling at bay.

Also consider fruit juice, vegetable juice, plain mineral water, or mineral water or soda pop made with artificial sweeter. You're also allowed up to two cups of skim milk on this program. Exercise restraint with soda pop or alcohol, which have no nutritional value. Soda pop is loaded with sugar, and alcohol is a relatively high-calorie, nutrition-free snack. It has 7 calories per gram, fewer than in fat but more than in carbohydrates and protein.

In fact, drinking alcohol works against losing weight, because spirits tend to enhance your appetite. Alcohol also dehydrates your body, which means that it's unwise to use it as a thirst-quencher during hot weather. Instead, replenish your body fluid with water, fruit or vegetable juice, or milk.

The USDA recommends that women limit themselves to a

maximum of one drink per day of alcohol (pregnant women should avoid alcohol). Men may have two drinks per day. This assumes "one drink" is a 12-ounce bottle of beer, 5 ounces of wine, or 1½ ounces of hard liquor. Beer labeled "light" contains fewer calories than the same brand of regular beer.

Organic Food: Is it Really Safer?

Organic fruits and vegetables, which are considerably more expensive than non-organic produce, have been grown from soil that has not been treated with pesticides or chemicals for at least three years. But there's nothing to stop the farmer in the field next door to an organic farm from using pesticides on his or her crops. In fact, there's no official regulatory process to protect consumers of organic products and no standard definition of "organic."

There are no additives, preservatives, or coloring in fresh American meat. Low levels of antibiotics are sometimes given to livestock to control or prevent disease, but the antibiotics are stopped for a period before slaughter.

There's no such thing as hormone-free meat. Like humans, animals naturally produce hormones, and they're given to some livestock in order to promote growth and to reduce the fat content of the meat.

Additives, preservatives, and coloring found in packaged or canned foods have been stringently tested for safety by the FDA. Though you should use fresh food as often as possible, don't hesitate to use packaged foods to add convenience to your nutritional intake. After all, if the only way you're going to eat a salad is with salad dressing and you don't have time to make your own, it's time to consider using bottled low-cal dressing. It'll make the salad taste better and you'll get the nutritional benefits of the fresh vegetables.

Save on Supplements

Can vitamin and mineral supplements help you to lose weight? There's a simple answer: no. If you follow our guidelines for weight loss, you're going to get all the vitamins and minerals you need from fat-burning foods and other sources. You don't need vitamin pills unless your doctor prescribes them to treat a specific condition.

There are two types of vitamins: fat-soluble (vitamins A, D, E, and K) and water-soluble (all others). Almost all foods contain some of the vitamins and minerals your body needs, so if you enjoy a variety of foods on this program, you should be getting all the nutrients you need. In fact, since your body can use vitamins and minerals only in small amounts, you excrete all the extra water-soluble ones in your urine. Excess fat-soluble vitamins are stored in your fat, may never be needed, and can become toxic if you take too many.

If you must take multivitamin supplements, take ones that contain iron and as broad a range of vitamins as possible, including all the B vitamins, in amounts not exceeding federally suggested limits.

Don't think that because a little is good, a lot would be better. When you get vitamins from your food, you get them in the minute amounts you need. Once you start taking megadoses from supplements, you're no longer taking a vitamin. You're taking a drug.

I've Got My Supplies: Now What Do I Do?

The shopping's done and now it's time to put it all together and create fabulous fat-burning meals. Preparation is the key to keeping food low in fat and rich in nutrients. Here are some tips.

Preparation Tips for Meats

➤ Trim fat from meat before and after cooking.

➤ Remove skin from poultry.

➤ Replace stuffings and breaded toppings or coatings with herbs and spices.

➤ Refrigerate overnight stews, soups, boiled meat, and chili. Then, skim the fat off the top and enjoy.

➤ Broil, poach, stew, or roast, rather than fry or sauté. If you must sauté, use no more than half a teaspoon oil, in a non-stick pan.

➤ When a recipe tells you to sauté the meat in butter and/or oil, cook it in wine instead. Try red wine with onions for red meats, white wine with tarragon for chicken or fish. Or, cook the meat in broth or tomato juice.

➤ To keep red meat as moist as possible, braise or stew. To keep natural juices in, avoid pricking or searing steaks.

➤ Marinades that include wine, vinegar, or lemon juice make meat more tender.

Preparation Tips for Vegetables, Pastas, and Grains

➤ Fill up on raw vegetables. They're better for you—and more filling—than cooked vegetables. They also take very little time to prepare and leftovers make great snacks.

➤ If you prefer vegetables with a cooked taste and texture, steam, stir-fry, broil, microwave, poach, or roast until they're barely tender. Avoid frying, basting, and sautéing.

➤ If you must boil vegetables, use the cooking liquid, which is where most of the nutrients end up, to make soup.

➤ Replace rich cream sauces with herbs, tomato sauce, or low-fat dressing.

➤ Make lasagna with low-fat cheese and/or cottage cheese, and lots of vegetables.

➤ Avoid rice mixes and fried rice. Season with herbs.

➤ Flavor baked potatoes with low-fat salad dressing or low-fat yogurt and herbs, not butter, margarine, mayonnaise, or sour cream.

➤ If a recipe tells you to sauté vegetables in butter or oil, cook them in wine. Mushrooms and onions are particularly delicious simmered in white wine.

Preparation Tips for Sandwiches

➤ Add flavor to low-fat cheese sandwiches by using a low-fat whole-grain bun, mustard, tomatoes, sprouts, and lettuce.

➤ Use lettuce and tomato, salsa, mustard, light mayonnaise, onion rings, or horseradish instead of butter or margarine.

➤ To moisten toast, use a little sugar-free jam or low-fat cream cheese instead of butter or margarine.

Fat-Burning Flavor Boosters

You can still enjoy many condiments and sauces to spice up your mealtimes. You can also use unlimited amounts of the following condiments and sauces to zip up your food. Buy low-sodium products whenever available, to prevent fluid retention. Try these flavor boosters:

Bouillon cubes	Mint sauce
Chili sauce	Mustards
Clear broth	Pickles
Cocktail sauce	Relishes
Cranberry sauce	Salsa
Herbs	Soy sauce
Horseradish	Spices
Ketchup	Steak sauce
Lemon juice	Sweet and sour sauces
Lime juice	Vinegars
Low-fat mayonnaise	Worcester sauce

The old days of creamy or oil-based dressings are now behind you. So are the days of butter, mayonnaise, sour cream, cheese, and cream sauces. Welcome to the world of herbs, mustards, lemon juice, vinegar-based dressings, diet salad dressing, non-fat yogurt, light sour cream, and whipped cottage cheese.

Here are a few tips on boosting flavor with condiments, sauces, and dressings:

➤ Fruit juices, vinegars, and herbs add zip to the flavor of dressings.

➤ Buttermilk, low-fat yogurt, and reduced-calorie mayonnaise can create creamy dressings.

➤ For cold salads, try reduced-calorie dressings or a specialty vinegar, such as balsamic or tarragon vinegar.

➤ Beer, wine, and tomato purée or broth, jazzed up with spices, make terrific marinades.

➤ Fruit juices or puréed fruits can replace sugar.

➤ Mustard and salsa can replace ketchup.

Enjoying Mealtimes

Breakfast—your most important meal

Study after study has shown that you run on empty when you wake up in the morning. You wouldn't jump in your car and go on a big trip without filling your gas tank. There's even evidence that the nutrients you miss at breakfast are never compensated for during the day. So why would you even consider starting your day without a good breakfast?

A good breakfast is also essential for safe and effective weight loss. One study in the Midwest showed that overweight people who received their entire allotment of calories at breakfast lost weight, while those who took in all their calories at dinnertime gained weight.

Break away from the expected, and eat leftovers from last night's dinner. Vegetables, lentil soup, or chickpea salad are just as nutritious in the morning as the night before. Or, try throwing a banana, low-fat yogurt, and orange juice in the blender, accompanied by sugar-free jam on toast for a quick-fix breakfast. A bowl of low-fat enriched cereal loaded with fruit and a bit of skim milk is not only convenient but rich in minerals and fiber.

Microwaveable oatmeal plus low-fat milk is a terrifically filling start to your day. Oatmeal has lots of high-quality protein compared to other grains, but is relatively low in fiber. To add fiber, throw in oat bran, wheat germ, or soy grits while the oatmeal is cooking.

Add fruit to cereal for flavor instead of butter, with low-fat milk. Add egg whites to eggs when making omelettes, beat in nonfat milk and flour to thicken the mix. Fill it with lots of vegetables.

Other alternatives include homemade waffles and pancakes, low-fat yogurt with cereal, low-fat cottage cheese combined with fresh fruit, a bagel or English muffin topped with Neufchatel or light cream cheese, homemade low-fat muffins, or fruit.

Lunch options

Some of the same people who skip breakfast also believe a quick lunch on the go will help them lose weight. They're wrong. Lunches on the go tend to be long on fat and short on satisfaction. Plan a fat-burning meal that you can enjoy, if only for 20 minutes.

Consider fresh fruit, grains, a sandwich of low-fat cheese, turkey or chicken breast, a fillet of fish with lettuce and tomato, sliced vegetables, or leftovers warmed up from dinner.

Our recipe section has a variety of low-fat sandwich fillings. No matter what sandwich filling you use, spice it up with low-fat mayonnaise, ketchup, salsa, or mustard rather than butter or margarine. If you're in a rush, consider beans on toast or cold rice salad.

If you're a soup fan, how about a huge bowl of noodle soup? A big bowl of chicken noodle soup (heavy on the noodles) will fill you up and keep you going. Dry soup to which you add water is also a good low-fat meal. Whatever soup you choose, stick to clear broths rather than cream soups.

Dinner à la thin

For most people, the temptation to overeat is strongest when the sun goes down. You're relaxed and perhaps a little tired after the challenges of your day, and stuffing yourself into oblivion looks appealing. Stop! There's nothing wrong with relaxing over a good dinner, but you're going to have to redefine your definition of "good dinner" to include plenty of fat-burning foods.

The section of this book on preparing protein is loaded with important tips on preparing and cooking poultry, fish, or red meat. In general, stop frying and start broiling, poaching, and roasting. And don't allow protein to be the star of the meal. Instead, splurge on relatively large portions of baked potatoes, whole grains, vegetables, salads splashed with low-fat dressing, and fruits. Eat dinner no later than 6 p.m., in order to give your body time to digest the meal before bedtime.

Get your snack attack on track

Try to stop snacking by 8:30 p.m. in order to give your body 11 or 12 hours to burn off all food before breakfast. The following foods are all fat-burning, low-fat treats. Exercise reasonable restraint, but enjoy them when you crave a treat.

Air-popped popcorn
Animal crackers
Bagels
Bread sticks
Canned or frozen fruit
Fat-free baked goods
Fig bars
Frozen fruit bars
Gelatin (regular or
    sugar-free)
Ginger snaps
Graham crackers
Hard candy
Hot cocoa mix (regular or
    sugar-free)

Ice milk
Melba toast
Non-fat yogurt
Non-fat frozen yogurt
    (plain or sugar-free)
Popsicles
Pretzels
Raw vegetables
Rice cakes
Saltine crackers
Sorbet
Tomato juice
Vanilla wafers
Vegetable juice

Seven-day Sample Menu

The sample menu on pages 94-95 provides a whole week's worth of ideas for fat-burning success. (See Chapter 4 for complete recipes.) These menus will get you started on the program. You can also develop your own recipes using what you have learned to keep them low in fat and high in complex carbohydrates.

Exercise: Fat-Burning in Action

As you have learned by now, what you put into your mouth is the most important component of this plan. But exercise is an amazing fat-burner as well. As you learned in the last chapter, **regular exercise keeps your metabolism high enough to burn off body fat. Exercise also encourages your body to burn fat instead of carbohydrate stores or muscle.**

Aside from helping you lose weight and keep it off, regular activity can:

➤ reduce stress and improve circulation and digestion,

➤ cut your risk of developing heart disease and diabetes,

➤ keep your bad blood cholesterol levels low, and

➤ just plain make you feel better.

There are many different types of exercise, but to maximize weight loss, choose aerobic activities. They provide a workout

SEVEN-DAY SAMPLE MENU

	Monday	Tuesday	Wednesday
Breakfast	orange	apple juice	grapefruit
	frozen waffle	corn meal muffin	fruit cocktail muffin
	hot cereal	oatmeal	farina
Lunch	pasta fagioli	Jamaican chicken	special turkey salad
	steamed asparagus	vegetable salad	Danish salad
	rutabaga bread	herbed biscuit	speckled brown bread
		banana	pear
Dinner	mixed Chinese vegetables	vegetable lasagna	shrimp & asparagus
	carrot-poppy seed bread	basic green salad	brown rice
	cool cucumber pasta salad		cucumber & onion salad
	apple-grape salad	three fruit sherbet	crocked acorn squash

Thursday	Friday	Saturday	Sunday
apple	melon	grapefruit	melon
carrot-oat muffin	frozen pancake	mini-bran fruitcake muffin	wheat-bran bread
prepared cereal	hot cereal	oatmeal	prepared cereal
Mexican stuffed pepper	lunch box minestrone	hot Chinese noodles	chunky chicken salad
famous bean salad	basic green salad	bean sprout salad	sprout soup
wheat bran bread	whole-wheat French bread	carrot-poppy seed bread	carrot salad
orange	apple	peach	cranberry applesauce
chicken w/ tomatoes & chickpeas	stuffed zucchini	monkfish kabobs	burrito bundle w/frijoles
potato bread	rice salad	rice pilaf	green rice
eggplant salad	gourmet peas	molasses oat muffin	
lemon sherbet	cranberry applesauce	apple-grape salad	pineapple-grape parfait

for your heart, lungs, and large muscle groups. Brisk walks, swimming, cycling, and fitness classes (if you're really ambitious) burn off fat, and are important preventives for heart disease—the largest killer in North America. Water exercises, such as aqua-aerobics, are also great fat-burners, providing people who have painful joints with a terrific cardiovascular workout.

You don't need to become a jock. **Regular, low-key, aerobic exercise will help you lose weight far more efficiently than high-powered workouts.** If you're older than forty-five, you must avoid high-impact aerobic activities, such as jogging and jumping. These force too much weight suddenly onto joints and the lower back. Also, take competitive sports with a grain of salt. They're hard on your system and are not necessary in order to lose weight. Your victory will be a slim new body, not first prize at the Boston Marathon.

It's not even necessary to get to the gym for a 30- to 45-minute cardiovascular workout three to five times a week. Find a half-hour once a week, mark it in your calendar, and set aside the time in your schedule for the next few months. Even if you can only commit yourself to a 30-minute walk, your waistline will reap the benefits.

The key word is balance. Just 90 minutes of walking or gardening per week for a 156-pound person can boost metabolism enough to roll off pounds and keep them off. If you're heavier, you need to spend even less time at these activities because you will spend more energy in burning off fat.

When you consider that the following modest activities are enough to keep your weight loss going, how hard would it be to incorporate some of them into your weekly routine?

➤ 1¹/₂ hours walking at a normal pace

➤ 1¹/₂ hours gardening, hedging

➤ 45 minutes of swimming, fast crawl

➤ 1 hour 50 minutes leisure bicycling, at 5.5 miles per hour

➤ 2 hours 20 minutes ballroom dancing

➤ 1 hour 20 minutes golf

➤ 1 hour cross-country skiing

➤ 1 hour tennis

➤ 2 hours 20 minutes volleyball

Better yet, make a point of doing something physical every day or at least every other day. And always choose activities you enjoy. Variety will make these activities fun and exhilarating!

Walking—fat-burning in motion

A brisk daily walk is the ideal exercise for most people. Injuries are unlikely, the only equipment you need is a good pair of shoes, and you can stay active anywhere, alone or with company.

The latest research shows that walking, at a moderate pace, is just as good a weight-loss strategy as a tough workout— maybe better. According to a study published by the *Journal of the American Medical Association,* a brisk 20-minute walk at least three times a week can help people live longer than any other form of exercise. As well, you'll be slim and fit during the years you add to your life.

Regular walking raises your metabolic rate just as effectively as attending an exercise class, which is what you need to continue your weight loss. What's critical is the amount of time you spend at it. You're far more likely to lose weight if you walk at a moderate pace for, say, 30 minutes a day, three times a week, than if you take an hour-long jog once a week. Walking for more than an hour a day doesn't seem to add to the benefits, either. Overdoing it isn't going to help you.

All you need is a good pair of walking shoes and comfortable clothing. Make sure your shoes have good arch support and adequate room for your toes. If you're walking in cold weather, cover the lower part of your face with a scarf, to avoid inhaling cold air into your lungs.

At first, you may want to walk slowly and just enjoy the scenery. Eventually, your pace should be brisk enough to carry on a conversation without having to catch your breath. For better back health, maintain good posture: hold your head up proudly, tuck in your pelvis, and straighten your back.

Exercise tips

Here are some easy ways to include regular exercise in your routine:

➤ Park the car a few blocks away from the office and walk the rest of the distance.

➤ Get off the bus one stop before the office and walk to work from there.

➤ Walk or run up the stairs to your office instead of taking the elevator.

➤ Take the kids to the park to play frisbee.

➤ Use your feet instead of the car. When you need to pick up some milk at the last minute, walk to the grocery store instead of driving.

➤ Use your bicycle instead of the bus.

➤ Start a garden or build a deck onto your house instead of having someone else do the work.

➤ Play hockey with your kids instead of sending them to Little League games.

➤ Use a regular broom instead of an electric broom to sweep floors.

➤ Help your neighbor bring in the hay this fall.

➤ Walk your children to school in the morning.

Eventually, you may become ambitious enough to set up an exercise program. Here's how to make it appealing:

➤ If you want to exercise at home, select a room or part of a room that you don't visit often. Decorate it with bright colors, which are stimulating. It will be invigorating just to walk in the room.

➤ To help time pass more pleasurably while you're exercising, listen to your favorite music or even watch television.

➤ Exercise with a partner or a group. Take a regular bike ride after dinner with a friend, or join a walking group.

➤ Motivate yourself with realistic short-term goals ("I'm going to bicycle to the grocery store for milk on Saturday mornings") as well as an achievable long-term goal ("by August, I'll be bicycling to work three times a week").

You're Off to a Great Start

You are now prepared to start slimming down. Focus on eating fat-burning foods, cutting fat and protein intake, and exercising regularly, and get ready to start taking in your clothing. Now that you've got the knowledge—and the tools to use that knowledge—nothing can hold you back!

CHAPTER 3

KEEPING IT OFF—
YOU CAN DO IT!

WITHIN A WEEK OR TWO ON THIS PROGRAM, you're going to feel so much better about yourself—and your waistline—that you won't believe the change! You'll have succeeded in replacing the irritability you felt in the old days, during one of your many starvation diets, with pride in your appearance.

Because fat-burning foods tend to be less expensive than fatty, processed, high-protein foods, the only weight-gainer around your place should be your wallet.

Although this program is easy and satisfying, it can be difficult to resist backsliding, especially once you've lost all the weight you need to lose. Social occasions, stress, the rush of modern life, and the difficulty in finding the "right foods" in restaurants are all challenges you will have to face on an ongoing basis.

Read on to learn valuable tips on coping with the challenge of keeping that weight off for a lifetime. You're worth it!

Satisfy the Party Animal in You

The party is in full swing and the canapé tray is loaded with tiny mouthfuls of temptation. Most people at parties stuff themselves with so much food they can't even estimate their intake! Studies have shown that many people will consume more than 2,000 calories of unnecessary food over the course of an evening! The trick is to prepare yourself beforehand.

Keep these suggestions in mind at the next party or social outing you attend:

➤ Don't skip lunch because you know you're going to be eating dinner out. You'll arrive starving and probably overeat.

➤ Before you leave for the party, eat some fruit or a jam sandwich so you don't arrive hungry.

➤ If you don't think there will be anything you can eat at the party, offer to bring fresh vegetables, along with a low-fat dip. Then, at the party, eat only your contribution.

➤ Try to eat slowly and enjoy your food.

➤ Drink lots of soda water, diet drinks, or fruit juice. (Note: If you choose a diet drink that has caffeine in it, such as Coke, expect to react as if you've drunk coffee.)

➤ Avoid the bar. Alcoholic beverages have no food value, and may impair your judgement about what to eat.

De-stress for Success!

Although you're going to feel and look better than ever, change is not easy. You're going to need the support of your family, friends, and co-workers, and you will have to work together to keep your motivation up. You're allowed to make mistakes! You're human. Don't be ashamed to ask for help.

Compulsive overeaters, however, may need more help than any one friend can offer. If it's within your budget, a few sessions with a therapist might help you understand why you overeat. Or, you may consider joining a support group, such as Overeaters Anonymous, which uses a twelve-step program in helping overeaters break their habits. Overeaters Anonymous is listed in your local phone book, or you can write P.O. Box 92870, Los Angeles, California, 90009, for information on the meeting place nearest you.

If you tend to overeat to cope with stress, depression, loneliness, or just plain boredom, turn to one of the alternative activities you learned about in the previous chapter. Take a walk, call a friend, or take up a hobby. It's far healthier to do something about your problems than it is to bury them under a mound of unhealthy food.

You may need to look more closely at managing your stress before you can stick to this amazing program. Stress can be a positive force, providing the extra spurt of energy you need to finish a job, the drive that keeps you going on an important project, or the enthusiasm to provide moral support to your family and friends.

The problem with stress is not so much the actual source— your mortgage, the traffic jam on the way home, your teenager's attitude—as how you deal with it. Everyone gets upset over major calamities. But if you are regularly using the small irritations of everyday life as an excuse to overeat, then you're giving stress too much power over your life—and your waistline.

Time management, career planning, or assertiveness training may help you feel calmer. Time management, for instance, offers practical techniques for scheduling activities so you don't feel rushed and out of control of your time and life.

Career planning could help you explore your skills, aptitudes, and interests, and to identify occupational choices that will satisfy your personal and professional ambitions. This will make you feel more in control of your own destiny.

Assertiveness training will teach you how to clearly communicate your opinions, ideas, and feelings, without backing down, in an effective, non-threatening way.

Progressive relaxation is another effective, easy technique for total body relaxation. It's a method of systematically tensing and relaxing your body, one part at a time.

Visualization is a method of creating a positive mental environment by imagining you have already achieved a specific, identifiable goal. The effectiveness of this technique for coping with serious illness has been widely promoted in books such as Dr. Bernie Siegel's best-seller *Love, Medicine, and Miracles.*

If you still can't relax, try breath control, self-hypnosis, yoga, meditation, tai chi, even listening to music or doing color-by-number paintings.

Check your local library or bookstore for self-help guides on these and similar topics, or ask about personal development courses or seminars at community centers, night schools, or other learning institutions.

Another way of reducing stress—and sticking to this program—is to plan ahead.

Help! Half an Hour Until Dinnertime!

What to do when you arrive home, kids in tow, with nothing in sight for dinner? Don't despair. A great weight-loss meal could be 30 minutes away, and the entire family will enjoy it. Here are a few tips to help you along the way:

➤ Store meal-sized portions of cooked rice, beans, peas, low-fat corn tortillas, broths, tomato sauce, and soups in your freezer. Stock up on frozen vegetables, cooked leftover chicken, turkey, pork, beef, veal, and fish. You can easily combine two or more portions into one satisfying meal, with a little help from your microwave.

➤ Take frozen chicken or meat out of the freezer in the morning to use as a satisfying touch of protein in a quick stir-fry. Cook up garlic, onions, ginger, soy sauce, and a little oil in a wok, throw in frozen vegetables and chopped up meat or tofu, and serve over rice or another grain.

➤ Likewise, fish poached in water and lemon juice, spiked with celery, carrots, and onions, cooks quickly. If it's not a strongly-flavored fish, you can drain the broth through a cheesecloth and freeze it. Fish broth is a great foundation for fish chowder, which is a fast fat-burning meal. Just add cooked carrots, onions, celery, potatoes, other vegetables of your choice, skim milk, and fish bits to the stock.

➤ Pastas are so fast and nutritious they should become a regular part of your "fast food" diet. While you're boiling the noodles, cook up garlic and onion in a little oil, and, in another pan, warm a can of plum tomatoes, frozen vegetables, and some oregano, basil, and pepper. Toss it all together, top with low-fat parmesan, and you have a meal in 15 minutes. Add a small quantity of ground meat, chopped meat, or canned fish if you want.

➤ Pasta primavera is an even faster meal. A few minutes before your dried pasta is cooked, throw in a bag of frozen mixed vegetables and cook until the vegetables have just thawed. Drain well, then toss with diet dressing and dust lightly with low-fat parmesan.

➤ Microwave-baked potatoes are fast, healthy vehicles for tasty fillings. Stuff with low-fat cottage cheese, low-fat yogurt, and broccoli, or cooked vegetables, a small amount of water-packed canned salmon, and a sprinkle of low-fat parmesan.

➤ Stock up on dehydrated refried beans and low-fat tortillas for another easy meal. Defrost the tortilla in the microwave, add water to the beans, and cook up some onions, pepper, and tomatoes in water. Stuff the tortilla with beans and vegetables, top with grated low-fat cheese, and you have burritos in five minutes.

➤ "Under-10-minute" alternatives to plain brown rice include quick-cooking barley, quick-cooking brown rice, bulgur, and couscous.

➤ Combine a can of beans with half a can of tuna, chopped peppers, onions, minced parsley, other fresh herbs, and a splash of low-fat salad dressing for a delicious, satisfying dinner on the go.

➤ Combine bite-sized pieces of chicken breasts, canned chicken broth, ginger, frozen vegetables, and egg noodles for a nourishing dinner soup.

➤ Marinate tofu in the refrigerator all day to jazz up its flavor, then put it under the broiler. Here's a marinade that's simplicity itself: a combination of 1 tablespoon fresh rosemary, 1 tablespoon olive oil, 1 tablespoon raspberry vinegar, and 1 teaspoon Dijon mustard.

➤ If you only have time to make complicated dishes on the weekend, make twice as much as you need and freeze one meal, to be enjoyed during the week.

➤ During barbecue season, replace skewered beef with tofu chunks that have been marinated all day in 1/4 cup soy sauce, 1/4 cup red wine, 3 tablespoons rice vinegar, 1 tablespoon sesame oil, a dash of hot pepper sauce, and 2 cloves of minced garlic.

Quick, Low-Fat Fixings From (Gasp!) the Convenience Store

If it's 30 minutes to dinnertime and you have no dinner fixings, don't despair. Just stop in at the corner store for some, or all, of these quick fixings:

➤ Low-fat canned soup, doctored with canned or frozen vegetables, rice, and beans, is a terrific meal-in-a-bowl.

➤ Pasta, prepared tomato sauce, and canned or frozen vegetables, topped with grated low-fat parmesan, can be your main course, followed by canned fruit (make sure it's packed in fruit juice or water, not syrup) for dessert.

➤ Liquid eggs, low-fat cheese, and lots of frozen vegetables make a tasty omelette.

➤ A rice casserole made with beans, tomato sauce, and water-packed tuna will satisfy any growling tummy.

➤ Skim milk can be the basis for low-fat custards, quiches, puddings, and blender drinks.

Fat-Burning Lunches— in the Bag!

A nutritious and filling lunch will keep you on track. Consider these suggestions:

➤ Stave off sandwich blahs by using your freezer to store a variety of ready-to-use breads and fillings: cut low-fat rolls or bagels in half and put them in the freezer. Freeze low-fat corn tortillas, pita bread, and sliced bread.

➤ Dinnertime leftovers can provide plenty of interesting sandwich fillings. Slice and freeze uneaten cooked chicken, fish, turkey, or tofu, along with cooked vegetables. The next morning, just grab them on your way out the door. Heat them in the office microwave, and spice them up with a fat-burning flavor booster.

➤ Stuffed pita bread can be more interesting than a plain old sandwich. To fill it, bring along containers of vegetables, water-packed tuna, broiled chicken, and diet dressing. That way, the pita won't be soggy by lunchtime.

➤ Whenever you prepare food, make extra and recycle it into lunches. Make extra dinner vegetables, which can be combined with diet dressing into appetizing lunchtime salads. Or cook extra noodles at dinnertime, and add canned water-packed tuna, broiled chicken, chickpeas, beans, tofu, vegetables, and dressing.

➤ If your office has a microwave oven, take along a thermos of soup prepared the night before, along with crackers or bread, and a fruit.

➤ Keep cut-up raw vegetables, such as celery, carrots, and cucumber, in a closed container in the fridge ready to be tossed into your lunch bag.

➤ Make low-fat muffins and cookies on the weekend to satisfy your lunchtime sweet tooth. Alternatively, take along fresh fruit, low-fat puddings, yogurt, or fruit salad.

➤ A box of crackers at your desk, combined with low-fat cheese, vegetables, fruit, and popcorn, is good for snacking.

Renovate Your Recipes for Easy Weight Loss

Chapter 4 contains meal suggestions and recipes that will stoke your flavor furnace and guarantee steady weight loss. But there's no need to toss out the rest of your cookbooks. Often, you can replace protein with carbohydrates, or at least a lower-fat protein. You can get most of the fat out of a recipe—or at least minimize it—without affecting the flavor that much. For example:

➤ Experiment with butter-flavored sprinkles such as Butter Buds. You probably won't taste the difference on popcorn or artichokes. In fact, air-popped popcorn, sprinkled with butter-flavored sprinkles and low-fat parmesan (plus a touch of garlic salt if you're feeling adventurous), is a terrifically satisfying late-night snack.

➤ A puréed boiled potato added to soup broth is a wonderful thickener.

➤ When baking cookies or cakes, experiment with fewer eggs, sugar, or fat than the recipe calls for.

The Recipe Renovation Guide offers a few other suggestions, just to get you started. Soon you'll be renovating all your recipes with ease and confidence.

RECIPE RENOVATION GUIDE

Replace	With
Ice cream	Sherbet or ice milk
Creamy soups	Clear soups
Creamy or oil-based salad dressings	Lemon juice, vinegar-based, or diet salad dressings
Butter, margarine, or oil	Broth, low-fat yogurt, light mayonnaise, fruit juice, or wine
Bacon, bologna, corned beef, hot dogs, liverwurst, pastrami, sausages, pepperoni, and salami	Sliced chicken or turkey and meat substitutes found in health food stores
Gravies made from meat drippings	Herbs, spices, and clear broths
Mozzarella, cheddar, and other hard cheeses	Cheeses made of non-fat or skim milk, including cottage cheese

continued →

Replace	With
Cream cheese	Neufchatel cream cheese, light cream cheese
Whole milk ricotta cheese	Skim ricotta
Whole milk	Buttermilk, low-fat, and non-fat milk
Dairy creamers	Low-fat milk or non-dairy creamers made without coconut oil
Sour cream	Low-fat yogurt
Chocolate	Cocoa powder mixed with non-fat milk
Hot chocolate mix	Non-fat dry milk powder, unsweetened cocoa powder, and sugar
Regular potato chips	Polyunsaturated potato chips
Eggs	Egg whites, liquid eggs
Mayonnaise	Low-fat yogurt, low-fat (light) mayonnaise

Avoid the Pitfalls of Dining Out

Eating out can pose a special challenge now that your eating habits have changed. You can't expect a restaurant to improvise a dish not on the menu, but you can politely request that your food be prepared and served the way you need it. After all, you're paying for food as well as service. These hints should help:

➤ Contact the restaurant in advance to ask about the food and if special requests are honored.

➤ Don't be embarrassed to order an appetizer or a half-portion instead of a full meal (or share a full portion with a friend).

➤ Don't be embarrassed to send food back to the kitchen if it's not prepared according to your specifications. You're the one paying for it.

➤ Indulge in the bread basket. Believe it or not, you'll lose weight if you fill up on breadsticks, rolls, French bread, pita bread, or toast that show up on your table before the meal— *as long as you pass on butter or any other high-fat spread.*

➤ Ditto to vegetable sticks. Stuff yourself with carrots, celery, and so on. Enjoy.

➤ Select small amounts of margarine made from corn, safflower, sunflower, soybean, cottonseed, or sesame oils. Better yet, use condiments like mustard or salsa.

➤ If you wish to order meat, fish or poultry, make sure it's steamed, prepared in its own juice, broiled, roasted, or poached. Once it arrives, trim visible fat off the meat or skin off the poultry.

➤ A fresh green or fruit salad, accompanied by several side dishes of vegetables, beans, pilafs, and other grains is a terrific fat-burning meal. If the restaurant has no fat-free salad dressing or sauce, ask for salad dressings and sauces to be served on the side, and use only small amounts, if any at all.

➤ Ask for low-fat yogurt to top your baked potato, instead of butter or sour cream.

➤ Choose clear broth soups, such as noodle, bean, or minestrone, instead of cream-based soups.

➤ Choose fresh fruit or sherbet for dessert.

➤ Ask for skim milk for your coffee instead of whole milk, cream, or non-dairy creamer, which are high in saturated fat.

➤ Avoid deluxe anything. It usually means extra fat.

➤ Avoid creamy, breaded, batter-dipped, or fried foods.

➤ Avoid casseroles and foods with heavy sauces.

➤ Ask for a doggie bag for food you can't eat.

➤ If the meal comes with several courses, some of which you

can't eat, order à la carte even if you have to pay extra for it.

➤ If your business requires you to take people to lunch, take your clients to restaurants that serve foods you can eat. Salad bars, buffets, and smorgasbords are a safe bet; you can make your own selection.

In a **fast food restaurant,** order:

➤ fruit or regular salad, with dressing on the side

➤ plain baked or mashed potatoes, topped with a small container of low-fat yogurt you bring yourself

➤ broiled chicken on an unbuttered roll, accompanied by lettuce and tomato

➤ noodle soup

➤ corn on the cob

➤ fruit juice

Sorry, but you're going to have to pass on the hot dogs, hamburgers, cheeseburgers, milk shakes, and french fries.

In an **Italian restaurant,** order:

➤ pasta with tomato or marinara sauce

➤ vegetables

➤ salad

➤ broiled fish or chicken

➤ mushroom spaghetti

➤ vegetable pizza with half the normal amount of cheese and extra herbs

In a **Mexican restaurant,** order:

➤ corn (not flour) tortillas

➤ rice

➤ beans (even refried beans aren't bad in moderation)

➤ broiled chicken

➤ salads

➤ chicken taco or tostada, made with a baked or steamed tortilla

➤ vegetarian burrito (a steamed tortilla filled with beans, rice, salsa, and a little cheese)

In a **Chinese restaurant,** order:

➤ stir-fried dishes

➤ lots of steamed rice

Most Chinese food is very high in fat. Choose another type of restaurant if possible.

In a **steakhouse,** order:

➤ plain baked potato

➤ vegetables

➤ salads

In a **French restaurant,** order:

➤ chicken breast or fish fillet, poached in wine

➤ steamed mussels

In a **Japanese restaurant,** order:

➤ yakimono (broiled seafood)

➤ soba soup (noodle soup in broth, accompanied by spinach,

bean sprouts, other vegetables, and a little chicken, beef, or tofu)

➤ sushi (vinegared rice rolled up with raw fish and vegetables inside a thin sheet of seaweed)

➤ rice

In a **Greek restaurant,** order:

➤ chicken shish kebab

➤ salad without feta cheese, anchovies, or olives, with dressing on the side

➤ plaki (fish cooked with tomatoes, onions, and garlic)

➤ pilaf or other rice dish

At the local **breakfast diner,** order:

➤ toast or English muffins and jam

➤ cereal with fruit and skim milk

➤ three or fewer pancakes, with syrup only

➤ fruit salad and cottage cheese

Keep on Moving!

Once you've become the slender person you always knew you were, you'll still want to continue your activity program. That's the only way your metabolism can stay high enough to keep weight off.

Studies of extremely overweight people show that pound for pound, they need one-third to one-half fewer calories to maintain their weight than people who are not overweight. The reason is, body fat needs fewer calories to maintain itself than lean muscle tissue.

Now that you have more muscle tissue than fat, you'll need regular activity to keep burning off excess calories before your body converts them into fat. As long as you stay active, you'll be able to eat as much as you want of the fat-burning foods on this program.

Final Words: Nip Temptation in the Bud

If you stick to the program outlined in this book, the pounds will melt away. Be patient, and watch the needle on the scale plunge downward gradually. If, however, several weeks go by and you're not losing weight, ask yourself these questions:

1. Have any excess fats "sneaked" onto your plate? If fried foods and buttered rolls have found their way back into your diet, or if you've stopped reading labels to track down hidden fats, the pounds will stop dropping off. Whether it's whole milk instead of skim milk or butter on your toast, get rid of it!

2. Are you stuffing yourself out of boredom? You should not be hungry on this diet, but you do have to stop eating when your stomach is full.

3. Have you kept your activity level up? Your daily walk or other routine is an essential component of your fat-burning program. If your life has suddenly become too busy for a regular walk, remember some of the other tricks suggested in Chapter 2. Park the car a couple of blocks away from the office, for instance, or use the stairs instead of the elevator at the office.

4. Have you kept your protein consumption down? If that weekly 3-ounce steak has become a fat-marbled 6-ouncer several times a week, the extra fat in your diet will keep you from losing weight. Instead, start filling up on carbohydrates.

5. What about your serving sizes? If you're basing your fat intake on the new labels but eating twice as much as the label serving size, you're deluding yourself.

Happy eating!

CHAPTER 4

MENUS AND RECIPES FOR FAT-BURNING SUCCESS

Seven-Day Menu

Day 1

Breakfast 1 sliced orange
1 low-fat frozen waffle
$^1/_2$ cup hot cereal

Lunch 1 serving Pasta Fagioli (page 167)
1 cup Steamed Asparagus (page 160)
1 slice Spicy Rutabaga Bread (page 142)

Dinner 1 serving Mixed Chinese Vegetables (page 165)
1 slice Carrot-Poppy Seed Bread (page 134)
1 cup Cool Cucumber Pasta Salad (page 149)
1 serving Apple-Grape Salad (page 175)

Snack 1 medium-sized pear

Day 2

Breakfast $3/4$ cup apple juice
                $1/2$ cup cooked oatmeal with cinnamon
                    and raisins
                1 Corn Meal Muffin (page 135)

Lunch   1 serving Quick Jamaican Chicken
                    (page 168)
                $1/2$ cup Marinated Raw Vegetable Salad
                    (page 153)
                1 Herbed Biscuit (page 136)
                1 banana

Dinner   1 serving Vegetable Lasagna (page 172)
                1 cup Basic Green Salad (page 145)
                $1/2$ cup Three Fruit Sherbet (page 178)

Snack $1/2$ cup grapes

Day 3

Breakfast	$^1/_2$ grapefruit
	1 Fruit Cocktail Muffin (page 135)
	$^1/_2$ cup farina
Lunch	1 serving Special Turkey Salad (page 170)
	1 slice Speckled Brown Bread (page 141)
	$^1/_2$ cup Danish Salad (page 150)
	1 medium-sized pear
Dinner	1 serving Shrimp and Asparagus (page 169)
	with $^3/_4$ cup short-grain brown rice
	1 cup Cucumber and Onion Salad (page 149)
	1 quarter Crocked Acorn Squash (page 177)
Snack	1 cup air-popped popcorn

Day 4

Breakfast   1 medium-sized apple
             1 Carrot-Oat Muffin (page 133)
             1 ounce prepared cereal with $1/4$ cup
                 non-fat milk

Lunch   1 Mexican Stuffed Pepper (page 164)
             $1/2$ cup Famous Bean Salad (page 152)
             1 slice Wheat Bran Bread (page 143)
             1 medium-sized orange

Dinner   1 serving Chicken with Tomatoes and
                 Chickpeas (page 163)
             1 slice Potato Bread with Caraway Seeds
                 (page 139)
             $1/2$ cup Eggplant Salad (page 151)
             1 serving Lemon Sherbet (page 177)

Snack   1 cup carrot sticks

Day 5

Breakfast   1 slice honeydew melon
1 low-fat frozen pancake
$1/2$ cup hot cereal

Lunch   1 cup Lunch Box Minestrone (page 155)
1 cup Basic Green Salad (page 145)
1 slice Whole-Wheat French Bread
  (page 144)
1 medium-sized apple

Dinner   1 serving Stuffed Zucchini (page 171)
$1/2$ cup Gourmet Peas (page 157)
$1/2$ cup Rice Salad (page 160)
1 cup Cranberry Applesauce (page 176)

Snack   1 slice cantaloupe

Day 6

Breakfast	$1/2$ grapefruit
	1 Mini-Bran Fruitcake Muffin
	    (page 137)
	$1/2$ cup cooked oatmeal with cinnamon
	    and raisins

Lunch	1 cup Hot Chinese Noodles (page 158) 1 serving Bean Sprout Salad (page 146) 1 slice Carrot-Poppy Seed Bread (page 134) 1 medium-sized peach
Dinner	1 serving Monkfish Kebabs (page 166) $3/4$ cup Rice Pilaf with Onion (page 159) 1 Molasses-Oat Muffin (page 138) 1 serving Apple-Grape Salad (page 175)
Snack	6 vanilla wafers

Day 7

Breakfast   1 slice melon
1 slice Wheat Bran Bread (page 143)
1 ounce prepared cereal with $1/4$ cup non-fat
   milk

Lunch   1 serving Chunky Chicken Salad (page 148)
1 cup Sprout Soup (page 156)
$1/2$ cup Carrot Salad (page 147)
$1/2$ cup Cranberry Applesauce (page 176)

Dinner   1 Burrito Bundle with Frijoles
   (pages 161 and 162)
1 cup Green Rice (page 158)
1 Pineapple-Grape Parfait (page 178)

Snack   1 slice Pumpkin Bread (page 140)

Bountiful Breads

Carrot-Oat Muffins

3/4	cup quick-cooking oats
1	cup low-fat buttermilk
1 1/4	cups unbleached flour
3	teaspoons baking powder
1/2	teaspoon salt
1	egg
3	tablespoons honey
1/2	cup carrots, finely shredded
1	teaspoon orange rind, grated

Combine oats and buttermilk in a mixing bowl and let stand for 15 minutes. Beat egg with honey. Meanwhile, combine flour, baking powder, and salt. Stir with egg into the oat mixture. Fold in carrots and orange rind, stirring only enough to moisten all ingredients. Spoon into muffin cups sprayed with low-fat cooking spray. Bake at 400°F for 20 to 25 minutes. Serves 12.

Carrot-Poppy Seed Bread

2	packages active dry yeast
1/4	cup lukewarm water
2	cups hot water
1/4	cup molasses
2	teaspoons salt
1/4	cup oil
2	cups carrot pulp
3	teaspoons poppy seeds
5 1/2	cups whole-wheat flour

In a small bowl, soften yeast in lukewarm water. Separately, combine hot water, molasses, oil, salt, carrot pulp, and poppy seeds in a large mixing bowl. Stir until well mixed, then stir in yeast mixture and blend thoroughly. Add flour, 1 cup at a time (retain 1/2 cup for kneading). When dough is well mixed, turn out on a floured board and knead for 6 to 8 minutes. (Dough will be slightly sticky.) Transfer to an oiled bowl, cover, and let rise until doubled in bulk, about 90 minutes.

Punch dough down and divide into two oblong or round loaves. Place in bread pans or on cookie sheet sprayed with low-fat cooking spray; cover and let rise for 30 minutes. Bake in a pre-heated oven at 425°F for 10 minutes. Then, reduce heat to 350°F and bake for 35 to 40 minutes, or until bread is nicely browned.

Corn Meal Muffins

1 package corn meal mix
1 cup cream-style corn
1 egg, beaten
  low-fat sharp cheese, grated, to taste
  pepper, to taste

Mix ingredients together, place in muffin tins sprayed with low-fat cooking spray. Bake at 425°F for 12 to 15 minutes. Serves 8.

Fruit Cocktail Muffins

1 8-ounce can fruit cocktail, well drained
1 3/4 cups flour, sifted
2 tablespoons sugar
2 teaspoons baking powder
3/4 teaspoon salt
1 egg, well-beaten
3/4 cup milk
1/3 cup vegetable oil

Sift dry ingredients into mixing bowl. Make a well in the center. Mix milk, egg, and oil, and add to dry ingredients. Stir quickly, just enough to moisten. Add the drained fruit cocktail. Fill non-stick or paper-lined muffin tins two-thirds full. Bake at 400°F for 25 to 30 minutes. Serves 12.

Herbed Biscuits

2 cups flour
3 teaspoons baking powder
  pinch of salt
1 teaspoon brown sugar
2 tablespoons dried parsley flakes
1 teaspoon dill weed
$1/2$ cup and 3 tablespoons margarine, softened
  water

Mix together dry ingredients. Cut in margarine until mixture has a coarse consistency. Add enough water to make a workable dough. Shape and place in a non-stick baking sheet. Bake at 400°F until tops are browned. Serves 8.

Mini-Bran Fruitcake Muffins

$1/2$ cup unsweetened applesauce
$1/2$ cup bran cereal buds
$1/2$ cup wheat cereal flakes
$1/3$ cup nonfat dry milk powder
 1 teaspoon baking soda
$1/2$ teaspoon baking powder
 1 tablespoon all-purpose flour
 2 tablespoons dried currants or raisins, or chopped
     dried-fruit mixed
 1 teaspoon rum or brandy flavoring, or vanilla extract
 1 teaspoon pumpkin pie spice, optional
    pinch of grated orange peel, optional

Combine all ingredients in a bowl and mix thoroughly.
Spoon into six paper-lined muffin tins, three-quarters full. Bake
in a preheated oven at 350°F for 25 minutes. Serves 6.

Molasses Oat Muffins

1 1/2   cup quick-cooking oats, toasted*
  1   cup all-purpose flour
  3   teaspoons baking powder
3/4   teaspoon salt
3/4   teaspoon cinnamon
1/3   cup dark brown sugar, firmly packed
  1   large egg
2/3   cup milk
1/3   cup molasses
1/3   cup oil

Toast oats.* In a medium bowl stir together the flour, baking powder, salt, and cinnamon; then stir in the sugar and toasted oats. In a small bowl, beat the egg until yolk and white are blended. Add milk and molasses, and beat to blend. Add these and the oil to the flour mixture, and stir until dry ingredients are moistened. Fill muffin tins (each 1/3 cup capacity) sprayed with low-fat cooking spray about two-thirds full. Bake in a preheated oven at 400°F until a cake tester inserted in center of muffin comes out clean, or about 15 to 18 minutes. Serves 12.

*To toast oats, spread 1 1/2 cups quick-cooking oats in an ungreased rectangular cake pan. Bake in a preheated oven at 350°F until golden brown, or about 14 to 18 minutes. Cool. Makes 1 1/2 cups.

Potato Bread with Caraway Seeds

 1   medium potato, peeled and diced
1 1/2 cups water
 1   package active dry yeast
 2   tablespoons sugar
 2   tablespoons margarine
 1/2 cup liquid eggs
1 1/2 teaspoons salt
 2   teaspoons caraway seeds
4 1/2 cups all-purpose flour

Place potatoes in small saucepan with water, cover and bring to boil, then reduce heat to low. Cook 10 to 12 minutes or until tender. Drain, reserving 1 cup of boiled potato water. Steam diced potatoes a few minutes in saucepan until dry; mash alone.

When potato water has cooled to lukewarm, pour into mixing bowl. Add yeast and stir until dissolved. Add mashed potatoes, sugar, shortening, eggs, salt, caraway, and 2 cups flour. Beat with electric mixer on low speed for 1 minute, scraping bowl frequently. Increase speed to medium; beat 2 minutes. Mix in enough remaining flour to form dough that can be easily handled. Turn out onto floured board; knead until smooth and elastic. Place in greased bowl and cover. Let rise in warm place until double in bulk, 60 to 90 minutes.

Punch down dough. Turn out onto floured board; form into round loaf. Lightly spray 2-quart round casserole with low-fat cooking spray. Place loaf in casserole and cover. Let rise until double in bulk.

Bake at 375°F for 30 to 35 minutes or until golden. Remove from casserole; cool on wire rack. Makes one large loaf.

Pumpkin Bread

    1   cup honey
    1   cup date sugar
    1   cup oil
    3   cups pumpkin purée
    1   cup dates, chopped
    1   cup walnuts, chopped
    1   teaspoon salt
    1   teaspoon cinnamon
    1   teaspoon ground cloves
    4   teaspoons baking soda
    2   cups unbleached white flour
 2$^1/_2$ cups whole-wheat flour
  $^1/_2$ cup wheat germ

Mix together honey, date sugar (available at health food stores), oil, pumpkin purée, chopped dates, chopped walnuts, salt, cinnamon, cloves, and baking soda. Add flour and wheat germ. Put into three loaf pans sprayed with low-fat cooking spray and bake for one hour at 350°F. Serve warm. Makes three loaves.

Speckled Brown Bread

1 1/2   cups flour
1 1/2   teaspoons salt
1 1/2   teaspoons soda
1   teaspoon baking powder
2   cups zante currants, seedless grapes, or raisins
1   cup wheat germ
3/4   cup yellow corn meal
3/4   cup regular oatmeal
1   cup low-fat buttermilk
1   egg
3/4   cup molasses
1/4   cup maple syrup
2   tablespoons vegetable oil

Sift flour, salt, soda, and baking powder in a large bowl. Add zante currants, wheat germ, corn meal, and oatmeal. Beat one egg lightly and add buttermilk, molasses, maple syrup, and vegetable oil. Add to dry mixture and stir until flour is moistened. Pour into a 9- by 5-inch loaf pan sprayed with low-fat cooking spray and floured. Bake at 350°F for one hour. Cool in pan 10 minutes before turning out. Makes one loaf.

Spicy Rutabaga Bread

  1 cup all-purpose flour
 2/3 cup sugar
 1/2 teaspoon baking soda
 1/4 teaspoon allspice, ground
 1/4 teaspoon cinnamon
 1/4 teaspoon nutmeg
 1/4 teaspoon salt or to taste
 1/4 teaspoon baking powder
  1 egg
 1/2 cup rutabaga, cooked and puréed
 1/4 cup vegetable oil

Spray an 8- by 4-inch baking pan with low-fat cooking spray, and line with wax paper. Combine flour, sugar, baking soda, allspice, cinnamon, and nutmeg, and mix well. In separate bowl, beat egg and add rutabaga and vegetable oil. Add moist ingredients all at once to dry ingredients. Stir just enough to blend. Pour into prepared pan and bake in oven preheated to 350°F for one hour, or until toothpick inserted in center comes out clean. Makes one loaf.

Wheat Bran Bread

$^1/_4$ cup warm water
1 package active dry yeast
2 tablespoons margarine
2 tablespoons brown sugar
1 teaspoon salt
1 cup skim milk, scalded
$^1/_2$ cup unprocessed wheat bran
3 cups whole-wheat flour

Place warm water in large bowl, sprinkle yeast over, and stir to dissolve. Let stand 5 to 10 minutes or until foamy. Add margarine, brown sugar, and salt to hot milk. Stir until margarine is melted, then let cool to room temperature.

Stir milk mixture into yeast until blended. Stir in bran and enough whole-wheat flour to make soft dough. Place dough on a lightly floured surface and knead in enough whole-wheat flour to make smooth dough. Knead until smooth and elastic. Place in bowl lightly sprayed with low-fat cooking spray, and turn to coat. Cover and let rise in a warm, draft-free place until doubled in bulk, about 90 minutes.

Spray an 8- by 4-inch loaf pan with cooking spray. Punch dough down. Shape dough into a loaf and place in prepared pan. Cover and let rise until dough reaches rim of pan.

Preheat oven to 375°F. Brush top of loaf with water and bake in preheated oven 30 to 35 minutes or until bread sounds hollow when tapped on bottom. Remove from pan and cool on wire rack. Makes one loaf.

Whole-Wheat French Bread

2 cups whole-wheat flour
1 1/2 cups all-purpose flour
2 teaspoons salt
1 package active dry yeast
1 2/3 cups warm water (105 to 115°F)
additional all-purpose flour for kneading

Combine whole-wheat flour, all-purpose flour, and salt in large bowl. Dissolve yeast in warm water. Add yeast to flour mixture; mix well with wooden spoon until dough no longer clings to sides of bowl. Turn onto lightly floured board; knead until smooth and elastic, about 10 minutes. Place in greased bowl; cover and let rise until double in bulk, about one-and-a-half hours. Punch dough down; cut dough in half.

Turn each half onto lightly floured board; sprinkle with flour. Roll each half into a 15- by 3-inch rectangle; dust off flour. Knead each half approximately 10 minutes. Then bring edges up and pinch together tightly. Carefully place loaves, pinched side down, on lightly floured baking sheet. Cover with cloth towel; let rise 45 minutes.

Cut three diagonal slashes, about one-fourth inch deep, in each loaf. Preheat oven to 450°F, and spray with water from a plant mister to create steam. Put loaves in oven; spray oven again to create steam. Bake until loaves sound hollow when tapped, about 25 to 30 minutes. Remove loaves from oven and spray lightly with water. Cool on racks. Makes two loaves.

Fresh Salads

Basic Green Salad

1 head lettuce or other greens
1 teaspoon salt
1 clove garlic, peeled
1 tablespoons olive oil
  freshly grated black pepper
2 tablespoons wine vinegar

Wash lettuce in cold water. Shake well; pat dry with paper towel. Put salt in bottom of large wooden salad bowl. Grind garlic into salt until half the clove is gone; discard the remainder. Tear lettuce into bite-sized pieces and drop into salad bowl. Pour olive oil over lettuce; toss gently until all the leaves are coated. Sprinkle pepper over lettuce, add vinegar, and toss.

Greens. Experiment with different greens: Bibb lettuce, leafy Romaine or escarole, curly chicory, tart endive, rich spinach, pungent watercress. For the crispiest salad greens, wash leaves gently, then pat dry with paper towels and refrigerate in plastic bags until ready to use.

Extras. The basic green salad is often perfect. But when "something extra" suits the meal, try these "extras": tomato wedges, sweet-onion rings, chopped green onion, green pepper rings, sliced cucumbers, sliced fresh mushrooms, artichoke hearts, broccoli, and cauliflower.

Bean Sprout Salad

1   pound fresh bean sprouts
$^1/_2$ pound fresh mushrooms, sliced
$^1/_4$ cup vegetable oil
2   tablespoons vinegar
     juice of one lemon
2   tablespoons soy sauce
1   teaspoon prepared mustard
$^1/_2$ teaspoon paprika
2   tablespoons pimento, chopped
1   teaspoon salt
$^1/_2$ teaspoon pepper
$^1/_2$ green pepper, chopped

Rinse sprouts under cold water and let drain. Rinse mushrooms and let dry.

Put oil, vinegar, lemon juice, soy sauce, mustard, paprika, pimento, salt, and pepper in a jar with a lid. Shake well.

Combine sprouts and mushrooms. Before serving, pour dressing over salad and toss. Serves 6.

Carrot Salad

3 cups carrots, grated (7 medium carrots)
$1/2$ cup raisins
1 cup non-fat yogurt
$1/4$ cup orange juice
1 teaspoon lemon juice

Combine carrots and raisins. Take $1/2$ cup of carrot-raisin mixture and blend with yogurt, orange juice, and lemon juice. Combine yogurt mixture with remaining carrot-raisin mixture and mix well. Chill, serve cold. Serves 6.

Chunky Chicken Salad

2	cups cooked white rice
1	16-ounce can of chicken broth
2	teaspoons lemon juice
$1/2$	teaspoon rosemary, crumbled
1	bay leaf
$1^1/2$	cups chicken, cooked and cut into chunks
1	6-ounce jar marinated artichoke hearts, undrained
$1/3$	cup green pepper strips
$1/3$	cup carrots, shredded
$1/4$	cup green onion, chopped
	lettuce
1	tomato or several cherry tomatoes

Prepare rice, substituting the canned chicken broth for the water called for in package directions. Add lemon juice, rosemary, and bay leaf. Cook for 45 minutes. Remove bay leaf. Combine chicken with artichoke hearts, green peppers, carrots, and onion. Toss chicken and vegetables in rice. Serve on leafy lettuce and garnish with tomato wedges or cherry tomatoes. Serves 4.

Cool Cucumber Pasta Salad

1   8-ounce box pasta
1   cucumber, diced
1   tomato, diced
3   stalks scallions, diced
    salt
    pepper
$1/2$ cup light mayonnaise

Boil pasta until soft. Rinse under cold water and drain. Add mayonnaise, diced vegetables, salt and pepper to taste. Refrigerate until 30 minutes before serving. Serves 4.

Cucumber and Onion Salad

4   medium cucumbers, thinly sliced
2   red onions, thinly sliced
    salt
1   cup water
1   cup vinegar
4   tablespoons sugar

In a 2-quart casserole, layer cucumbers, then onions. Sprinkle with salt. Repeat layers and salt. Cover tightly and drain off liquid every hour for three hours. Combine water, vinegar, and sugar. Cover vegetables and refrigerate overnight. Serves 6.

Danish Salad

Salad:
- 1 16-ounce can French-style green beans
- 1 16-ounce can small tender peas
- 6 stalks celery, chopped
- 1 large onion, chopped
- 1 small can pimento, chopped

Dressing:
- 2 cups vinegar
- 1 tablespoon water
- 3/4 cup sugar
- 1 teaspoon salt
- 3/4 teaspoon pepper

Combine beans, peas, celery, onion, and pimento in large salad bowl. Mix vinegar, water, sugar, salt, and pepper, and pour over salad. Marinate 24 to 48 hours before serving. Serves 8.

Eggplant Salad

1 medium eggplant
1 tomato, chopped
1/4 green pepper, chopped
1/4 onion, chopped
   pepper, to taste
   vinegar, to taste

Bake eggplant at 350°F for 45 minutes or until soft. Cool. Cut lengthwise, scoop out insides, and chop. In a large bowl, mix eggplant with tomato, green pepper, onion, pepper, and vinegar. Chill. Serve on crackers or bed of lettuce. Serves 4.

Famous Bean Salad

1 8-ounce can green beans
1 8-ounce can wax beans
1 8-ounce can kidney beans
1 can chickpeas
1 2-ounce jar pimentos
1 cup onion, finely sliced
1 cup celery, sliced
1 cup vinegar
1 teaspoon salt
1 cup sugar, or substitute

Heat vinegar, salt, and sugar in a small saucepan. Cool. Set aside. Drain beans, chickpeas, and pimentos. Combine with onion and celery. Add vinegar mixture. Cover and refrigerate before serving. Serves 8.

Marinated Vegetable Salad

Salad:

4   small zucchini
2   small yellow squash
1/2   head broccoli
1/2   head cauliflower
2   small carrots
1   red onion
1/2   pound fresh mushrooms

Dressing:

1   cup white vinegar
1/2   cup wine vinegar
1/4   cup lemon juice
     salt, to taste
1/2   teaspoon oregano leaves
1/2   teaspoon dry mustard
1/2   teaspoon garlic powder
1/4   teaspoon anise seed

Slice salad vegetables and place in a large bowl. Combine all dressing ingredients in large jar. Shake well and pour over vegetables several hours before serving. Refrigerate. Stir once every hour. Serves 8.

Nutritious Soups

Lunch Box Minestrone

2	tablespoons olive oil
1/4	cup celery
1/4	cup onion
1/4	cup zucchini
1/4	cup carrots
1	small clove garlic, minced
3/4	cup cabbage, shredded
1	cup tomatoes, peeled, seeded, and chopped
2	teaspoons fresh basil, chopped (or 1/2 teaspoon dried)
2	teaspoons fresh oregano, chopped (or 1/2 teaspoon dried)
1/4	cup small pasta
3	cups beef broth
3/4	cup chickpeas
	grated Parmesan cheese, to taste

Dice celery, onion, zucchini, and carrots. Steam vegetables with garlic and cabbage until tender, but not brown. Add remaining ingredients except chickpeas and cheese and simmer 15 minutes. Add chickpeas and simmer another 5 minutes. Stir in a dash of grated Parmesan cheese. Serves 6.

Sprout Soup

1	medium potato, cut into chunks
1	medium carrot, cut into chunks
1	small onion, diced
1	stalk celery, chopped
1	cup vegetable or chicken stock
1/4	teaspoon salt
	dash of pepper
2	cups sprouts, coarsely chopped
2	tablespoons soy sauce
2	tablespoons parsley, chopped

Cook potato, carrot, onion, and celery in stock for about 10 minutes. Add salt and pepper. Process in blender until thick and smooth. Return to saucepan; add sprouts and soy sauce and simmer for 3 minutes. Garnish with parsley and serve immediately.

Savory Side Dishes

Gourmet Peas

2	cups peas, fresh or frozen
1	teaspoon onion, finely chopped
1/2	teaspoon mint leaves, dried and crushed
	watercress
	fresh mushrooms, to taste
2	tablespoons white wine

Combine peas, onion, and mint leaves in a saucepan. Cook in lightly salted water until just tender. Sauté fresh mushrooms in white wine. Add mushrooms and a handful of snipped watercress to drained, cooked peas just before serving. Serves 4.

Green Rice

$3/4$ cup green onions with tops, thinly sliced
$1/2$ cup green pepper, finely chopped
1 cup rice, uncooked
$1/4$ cup parsley, snipped
1 teaspoon salt
$1/4$ teaspoon pepper
2 cups chicken broth, boiling

Steam onions and green pepper over boiling water until soft but not brown. Place rice in a 2-quart baking dish. Add steamed vegetables, parsley, seasoning, and broth. Stir. Cover with tight-fitting lid or heavy-duty foil. Bake at 350°F for 25 minutes or until rice is tender and liquid is absorbed. Toss lightly with a fork before serving. Serves 6.

Hot Chinese Noodles

1 pound medium spaghetti or linguini, cooked and cooled

Garlic Ginger Mix:
12 garlic cloves
3 inches ginger roots
$3/4$ teaspoon salt
4 to 5 tablespoons water

Chop garlic and ginger, and mash with water and salt. Stir Garlic Ginger Mix into linguini. Serves 4 to 6.

Rice Pilaf with Onion

2   tablespoons olive oil
1   cup long-grain or converted rice, uncooked
2   cups chicken broth, or 2 cups hot water and
        2 teaspoons chicken-broth granules
2   tablespoons green onion tops, thinly sliced
1/8   teaspoon garlic powder

Heat oil in a medium-sized saucepan over medium-low heat. Add rice and cook until golden in color, stirring occasionally. Meanwhile, heat chicken broth to boiling, and add to rice. Add green onion tops and garlic powder. Cover and simmer for 25 minutes or until all liquid is absorbed. Fluff rice with a fork, and serve. Serves 4.

Rice Salad

4   cups cooked rice
1   chicken bouillon cube
1/2   cup onion
2   tablespoons vinegar
2   teaspoons salt
3/4   cup green pepper
2   cups celery
1   cup green peas, cooked
1   small jar pimento, chopped

Cook rice according to package directions, adding chicken bouillon cube to water. Mince onion in food processor. Mix together rice, onion, vinegar, and salt. Refrigerate for three hours or overnight. Mince green pepper and celery in food processor. Add to rice mixture along with peas and pimento. Serves 6.

Steamed Asparagus

1   pound fresh asparagus

Place raw asparagus standing up in a tall steamer. Pack enough asparagus to nearly fill the diameter of the steamer basket. Add water to boiler and drop basket in boiler. Bring water to a boil and cook until the lower part of the asparagus stems are just tender. Serves 4.

Exciting Entrees

Burrito Bundles with Frijoles

$^1/_2$ cup frijoles (see recipe on page 162)
$^1/_2$ cup onion, chopped
1   8 $^3/_4$-ounce can whole kernel corn, drained
4   10-inch corn tortillas
1   cup green pepper, diced
1 $^1/_2$ cups lettuce, shredded
1 $^1/_2$ cups low-fat sharp Cheddar cheese, shredded

Brown onion. Add corn and heat through. Place tortillas between two damp tea towels and warm in oven at 300°F for 3 to 5 minutes or until soft. Divide frijoles, corn, pepper, lettuce, and cheese among tortillas; fold envelope-style to eat. Serves 4.

Frijoles

2 1/2   cups pinto, black, or red kidney beans
2   onions, finely chopped
2   cloves garlic, chopped
1   bay leaf
2   or more serrano chiles, chopped, or 1 teaspoon dried
      pequin chiles, crumbled
1   tablespoon vegetable oil
1   medium tomato, peeled, seeded, and chopped

Wash beans, but do not soak. Put in cold water to cover. Add bay leaf, chiles, and half of the chopped onions and garlic. Cover and simmer gently, adding more water as needed. When beans begin to wrinkle, add oil. When beans are soft and almost done, add seasonings. Cook another 30 minutes without adding more water; there should be little liquid remaining when beans are cooked.

Steam remaining onion and garlic until limp. Add tomato and cook for 1 to 2 minutes; add a tablespoon of beans and mash into the mixture. Add a second tablespoon of beans without draining so that some of the bean liquid evaporates in this cooking process. Add a third tablespoon of beans without draining and continue to cook until the mixture becomes a smooth, fairly heavy paste. Return mixture to the bean pot and stir into beans over low heat, thickening the remaining liquid. Serves 6 to 8.

Chicken with Tomatoes and Chickpeas

1	pound boneless chicken breasts
2	tablespoons olive oil
1/2	pound mushrooms, sliced
1	8-ounce can chickpeas
1	tomato, chopped
1	green pepper, chopped
2	cloves fresh garlic, minced
1	teaspoon paprika
3/4	cup white wine
2	pinches of salt
2	pinches of black pepper

Boil chicken for 15 minutes. Drain. Let cool and slice into bite-sized pieces.

In a large cast iron skillet, add olive oil, chicken, mushrooms, chickpeas, tomatoes, green pepper, garlic, and paprika. Cook for 30 minutes. Add salt, black pepper, and white wine, and cook for a few more minutes, then serve. Serves 4.

Mexican Stuffed Peppers

6 large green peppers
1 pound lean ground beef
1 medium-size onion, sliced
2 cups crispy rice cereal
$1/8$ teaspoon minced garlic
2 teaspoons chili powder
1 teaspoon salt
$1/8$ teaspoon pepper
1 teaspoon sugar
1 6-ounce can tomato paste
1 16-ounce can peeled whole tomatoes, drained
$1/2$ cup (2 ounces) sharp Cheddar cheese, shredded

Wash peppers. Cut off tops and remove seedy portions. Precook in large amount of boiling water about 5 minutes. Drain well. Place peppers, cut side up, in shallow non-stick baking pan sprayed with low-fat cooking spray. Set aside.

Place ground beef and onion in a large skillet. Cook over medium heat, stirring frequently, until ground beef is browned. Drain excess drippings. Stir crispy rice cereal, garlic, chili powder, salt, pepper, sugar, tomato paste, and tomatoes into ground beef mixture, cutting tomatoes into pieces with spoon. Remove from heat. Spoon mixture into peppers, dividing evenly.

Bake at 350°F for about 20 minutes or until filling is thoroughly heated. Remove from oven. Sprinkle tops with cheese. Return to oven, and bake about 5 minutes longer or until cheese begins to melt. Serves 6.

Mixed Chinese Vegetables

 5 large Chinese mushrooms, dried
 1 cup lukewarm water
3/4 cup green cabbage
1/2 cup carrots
1/2 cup cucumber
 1 6-ounce can bamboo shoots
 2 tablespoons sesame-seed oil
1/4 cup frozen peas
1/2 cup hot chicken broth
 2 tablespoons soy sauce
    pinch of sugar

Soak mushrooms in water for 30 minutes. Shred cabbage; cut carrots, cucumber, and bamboo shoots into julienne strips. Cube mushrooms. Heat oil in skillet. Add cabbage and cook for 2 minutes. Add mushrooms, cucumbers, carrots, bamboo shoots, and peas. Pour in chicken broth. Season with soy sauce and sugar. Simmer over low heat for 15 minutes. Serve immediately. Serves 2.

Monkfish Kebabs

1 pound monkfish fillets, cubed
2 tablespoons vegetable oil
2 tablespoons dry white wine
1 clove garlic, peeled and finely chopped
1 tablespoon lemon juice
  salt and pepper to taste
1/2 teaspoon thyme
1/2 teaspoon oregano
2 onions, cut into chunks
2 green peppers, cut into 2-inch pieces
8 cherry tomatoes
1 zucchini, sliced

Place monkfish in shallow dish. Combine oil, wine, garlic, lemon juice, salt, pepper, thyme, and oregano in bowl and pour over monkfish. Refrigerate for at least one hour.

Drain monkfish; reserve marinade. Place fish, onions, green peppers, tomatoes, and zucchini on eight skewers. Place skewers in shallow baking dish. Pour reserved marinade over skewers, cover, and refrigerate for three hours.

Preheat broiler. Drain skewers; reserve marinade. Place skewers on broiler pan and broil for 8 to 10 minutes, or until fish and vegetables are tender. Baste with reserved marinade; turn skewers frequently. Place skewers on serving platter; serve on or off skewers. Serves 4.

Pasta Fagioli

$1/3$ cup pinto beans
$1/3$ cup kidney beans
$1/3$ cup Great Northern or white beans
3   onions, chopped
4   stalks celery, chopped
4   teaspoons parsley
1   8-ounce can tomatoes
1   pound trimmed chuck steak, cut into chunks
    Italian seasoning to taste
    garlic powder to taste
    water
    large meat bone
1   cup farfalle (bow tie) pasta

Soak beans overnight and drain. Brown meat, onions, and celery. Add tomatoes, meat bone, parsley, salt, pepper, Italian seasoning, garlic powder, beans, and 2 quarts water. Cook at least two hours. Remove bone. Add pasta and cook 10 minutes more. Best if marinated one day before eating. It may need to be thinned by adding 1 cup boiling water and a dissolved bouillon cube. Serves 4.

Quick Jamaican Chicken

1   chicken breast, split
2   tablespoons crushed corn flakes or cracker meal
     salt (or garlic salt)
     pepper to taste
3/4 cup tomato juice
4   tablespoons scallions or onions, finely chopped
       (or 1 tablespoon instant onion)
1/2 teaspoon allspice, ground
     pinch of thyme, ground
     pinch of hot pepper

Moisten chicken with water. In a plastic bag, shake chicken with crumbs, salt, and pepper. Place chicken skin side down in a small non-stick pie pan that has been sprayed with cooking spray for no-fat frying. Place pan, uncovered, in an oven pre-heated to 450°F. Bake 15 minutes; turn chicken skin side up and bake another 15 to 20 minutes until skin is golden-crisp and well rendered of fat. Drain and discard fat.

Combine tomato juice with remaining ingredients and pour over chicken. Lower heat to 350°F. Bake, basting often, until chicken is tender and sauce is thick (add water if sauce simmers away). Remove skin before serving. Serves 2.

Shrimp and Asparagus

1 pound shrimp, shelled, deveined, and cooked
1 6-ounce can medium chestnuts, drained and sliced
1 medium onion, sliced
1 cup fresh mushrooms, sliced
1 cup celery, sliced diagonally
1 4-ounce can mandarin oranges, drained
1 1/2 pounds fresh asparagus, steamed
2 tablespoons oil
1/4 teaspoon salt
1/2 teaspoon black pepper, freshly ground
2 tablespoons sugar
2 tablespoons soy sauce
3 cups rice, cooked

Prepare shrimp and set aside. Drain and slice water chestnuts. On a large tray arrange shrimp, chestnuts, onion, mushrooms, celery, mandarin oranges, and asparagus.

Heat oil in a wok. Add onion, celery, salt, pepper, and sugar. Stir-fry until vegetables are tender, but still on the crisp side. Add asparagus and shrimp. Place water chestnuts and mushrooms over shrimp. Sprinkle with soy sauce and place orange sections on top. Cover and cook until mixture steams. Serve with rice. Serves 4.

Special Turkey Salad

1	14-ounce cooked turkey breast, cut into strips
1 1/4	cups celery
2	yellow peppers, seeded and cut into strips
1	small onion, grated
1/4	cup low-fat mayonnaise
1	6-ounce container plain low-fat yogurt
2	teaspoons hot mustard
2	teaspoons maple syrup
1/2	teaspoon salt
1/8	teaspoon pepper
	green celery tops for garnish

Mix turkey, celery, and yellow peppers together in bowl. Mix grated onion with mayonnaise, yogurt, mustard, maple syrup, salt, and pepper. Toss turkey mixture in dressing, cover, and let stand at room temperature for 10 minutes before serving. Garnish with green celery tops and serve. Serves 4.

Stuffed Zucchini

2 zucchini squash
2 cups mushrooms, chopped
1 cup onion, chopped
2 cloves garlic, crushed
2 tablespoons dry white wine
1/4 cup parsley, chopped
1/2 teaspoon basil or thyme
   pepper to taste
1 teaspoon tamari sauce
1 cup non-fat cottage cheese
3/4 cup cooked brown rice (or millet or bread crumbs)

Slice zucchini in half lengthwise. Cut out center with a knife or spoon, leaving about 1/4-inch skin thickness all around. Place zucchini shells in a large pan and add a little water. Steam for 5 minutes. Sauté mushrooms, onion, and garlic in wine in a sauté pan for a few minutes. (Add the zucchini insides if you want.) Add parsley, basil, pepper, and tamari, sautéing several more minutes.

Turn off heat, add cottage cheese and rice, and mix well. Let mixture sit a few minutes. Drain mixture through a colander, saving liquid for later. Fill zucchini with vegetable-cheese mixture. Lay zucchini on a baking dish, and bake for 30 minutes at 350°F. Place drained liquid in saucepan, heat. To thicken, add a little cornstarch or arrowroot and cold water to the sauce. Cook sauce lightly to thicken, stirring often. Spoon sauce over zucchini and serve. Serves 4.

Vegetable Lasagna

 4   medium zucchini, coarsely chopped
 1   large onion, chopped
 1   medium green pepper, chopped
 1   carrot, finely chopped
 1/2 cup celery, chopped
 2   garlic cloves, minced
 1/4 cup olive oil
 2   16-ounce cans tomatoes in tomato sauce
 1   8-ounce can tomato sauce
 1   6-ounce can tomato paste
 1/4 cup dry white wine
 2   tablespoons parsley, finely chopped
 2   teaspoon oregano
 1   teaspoon basil
 1   teaspoon salt
 1/2 teaspoon thyme
 1/4 teaspoon pepper
 9   wide curly lasagna noodles, cooked
 2   cups (1 pound) part-skim ricotta cheese
 10 ounces skim mozzarella cheese, shredded
 1/2 cup Parmesan cheese, grated

In a large skillet, cook zucchini, onion, green pepper, carrot, celery, and garlic in oil over medium heat for 15 minutes, stirring frequently. Stir in tomatoes, tomato sauce, and tomato paste; add seasonings. Bring to a boil, stirring to break up tomatoes. Reduce heat, cover, and simmer 30 minutes. Uncover and boil to reduce sauce to about 5 cups.

In an $11^1/2$- by $9^1/2$-inch baking pan, spread about one fourth of the sauce over bottom of pan. Arrange three noodles on top; dot with one-third of the ricotta; then sprinkle with one-fourth of the mozzarella and one fourth of the Parmesan. Repeat procedure twice. Spread remaining sauce over all; top with remaining mozzarella and Parmesan. Bake at 350°F for 30 to 45 minutes. Let stand 5 minutes before serving. Serves 8.

Delicious Desserts

Apple-Grape Salad

2 medium tart apples, peeled, quartered, cored
1/2 pound blue grapes, halved, seeded
1 stalk garden mint (leaves only)
2 teaspoons sugar
2 tablespoons lemon juice

Cut apples crosswise in thin slices. Arrange grapes, apples, and mint leaves in glass bowl. Sprinkle with sugar and lemon juice. Toss lightly, then cover. Chill one hour before serving. Serves 4.

Cranberry Applesauce

  5 pounds red apples (about 25 apples)
$3/4$ cup water
  1 pound cranberries
$1^1/4$ cups sugar, more or less, depending on sweetness
     of apples

Wash apples; cut into quarters. (Do not peel or core.) Place water and quartered apples in large Dutch oven (5- or 6-quart size).

Wash cranberries; place on top of apples. Cover; bring to boil over medium heat. Lower heat; cook until apples lose their shape and are tender, about 30 minutes. Stir occasionally to prevent sticking and to allow apples to cook uniformly. When apples and cranberries are cooked, remove from heat. Press through food mill or blend until desired consistency. Sweeten with sugar to taste. Serve applesauce warm or chilled. Extra applesauce can be frozen or canned. Serves 6.

Crocked Acorn Squash

2   acorn squash
1/2 cup apple juice or cider
     cinnamon (or pumpkin pie spice)

Cut squash into quarters and scrape away seeds. Place squash in a crock cooker skin-side down. Pour 1/4 -cup to 1/2 -cup apple juice over squashes and sprinkle very lightly with ground cinnamon. Cover and cook on low setting two to four hours. Serves 8.

Lemon Sherbet

1 1/2 teaspoons unflavored gelatin
   2   tablespoons cold water
   2   cups skim milk
 3/4   cup sugar
 1/2   cup lemon juice
 1/2   teaspoon lemon rind, grated
   2   egg whites, stiffly beaten

Soak gelatin in water several minutes. Heat milk. Add sugar and gelatin; stir until dissolved. Chill in refrigerator until just firm. Gradually stir in lemon juice and rind. Pour into freezer-safe tray or bowl and freeze until slushy. Turn into chilled bowl; beat with electric beater until fluffy but not melted. Fold in beaten egg whites. Return to freezer and freeze until firm. Serves 6.

Pineapple-Grape Parfaits

2¹/₂ cups seedless green grapes, halved
1 8-ounce can crushed pineapple, drained
¹/₄ cup brown sugar
dash of ginger
1 cup low-fat vanilla yogurt

Reserve 6 grape halves for topping. Combine grapes and pineapple. In a separate bowl, stir brown sugar and ginger into yogurt. Alternately spoon fruit mixture and yogurt mixture into 6 parfait glasses, starting with fruit and ending with yogurt. Place reserved grape halves on top of each parfait. Chill at least 3 hours before serving. Serves 6.

Three Fruit Sherbet

2 bananas
³/₄ cup orange juice
¹/₃ cup lemon juice
1 egg
1 cup powdered sugar
1 cup skim or evaporated milk

Place all ingredients in electric blender and beat until smooth, about 1 minute. Pour fruit mixture into ice cube tray and freeze until firm. Serves 6.

Variation: Instead of bananas, use 4 to 5 medium-sized peeled pears or 1 medium melon.

Refreshing Beverages

Apple-Pineapple Cooler

3 cups unsweetened apple juice
2 cups unsweetened pineapple juice
1 cup orange juice
2 tablespoons freshly squeezed lime or lemon juice
  orange slices to garnish

Combine juices and orange slices; chill. Garnish glasses with orange slices. Serves 6.

Fruit Tea Punch

2 cups boiling water
4 black-tea bags
1/4 cup lemon juice
2 cups orange juice
1 tablespoon honey
1 lemon
2 oranges
2 cups fresh strawberries
1 bottle soda water

Pour boiling water over tea bags. Steep 3 minutes; remove tea bags. Blend in lemon and orange juice; sweeten with honey. Cut peel from lemon and oranges; section fruit. Remove all membranes. Add to tea. Wash and hull strawberries; cut in half; add to tea. Cover and refrigerate punch at least six hours to blend flavors. Just before serving, add bottle of soda water. Serves 10.

REFERENCES

Barnard, Neal. *Food for Life*. New York: Harmony Books, 1993.

Barnard, Neal. *Foods That Can Cause You To Lose Weight*. McKinney, Texas: The Magni Group, 1992.

Bennion, Lynn, Edwin L. Bierman, and James M. Ferguson. *Straight Talk About Weight Control*. New York: Consumer Reports Books, 1991.

Bricklin, Mark, and Claire Gerus. *Prevention's Lose Weight Guidebook*. Emmaus, Pennsylvania: Rodale Press, 1994.

Bricklin, Mark, and Sharon Stocker. *Prevention's Medical Healing Yearbook*. Emmaus, Pennsylvania: Rodale Press, 1991.

Brody, Jane. *Jane Brody's Nutrition Book*. New York: W. W. Norton & Co. Inc., 1981.

Consumers Guide, ed. *Cholesterol: Your Guide for a Healthy Heart*. Lincolnwood, Illinois: Publications International Ltd., 1989.

MacDonald, Helen Bishop, and Margaret Howard. *Eat Well, Live Well: The Canadian Dietetic Association's Guide to Healthy Eating.* Toronto: MacMillan, 1990.

Moquette-Magee, Elaine. *Fight Fat & Win!* Minneapolis: CHRONIMED/DCI Publishing, 1990.

Ornish, Dean. *Stress, Diet & Your Heart.* New York: Henry Holt & Co., 1982.

Schwartz, Rose. *The Enlightened Eater.* Toronto: Stoddart Publishing Co. Ltd., 1989.